The Unbroken Road

Katy Isaacs

Energion Publications
Gonzalez, FL
2014

Unless otherwise noted, all Scripture quotations are taken from the Holman Christian Standard Bible®, Copyright © 1999, 2000, 2002, 2003, 2009 by Holman Bible Publishers. Used by permission. Holman Christian Standard Bible®, Holman CSB®, and HCSB® are federally registered trademarks of Holman Bible Publishers.

Cover Image: ID 28894020 © Brett Critchley | Dreamstime.com
Cover Design: Henry Neufeld and Kathryn Brown Isaacs
Chapter Header Image: Kandace Brown

ISBN10: 1-63199-050-0
ISBN13: 978-1-63199-050-2
Library of Congress Control Number: 2014945833

Energion Publications
P. O. Box 841
Gonzalez, FL 32560

energionpubs.com
pubs@energion.com
850-525-3916

TABLE OF CONTENTS

To my family,
past, present, and future,
who are walking this journey with me
and who lovingly remind me to keep my eyes on Jesus.

1 Introductions

I turned the corner. The aisle stretched before me as the music escalated. My white slippers brushed over the red roses. My heart thumped. I had waited so long for this moment. Had I really made it this far? Hundreds of eyes twinkled their approval. But did they really think I was crazy? I could almost hear the question I had been asked before, "Do you think it will be worth the wait?" Here I was at this pinnacle moment.

My first kiss was only minutes away. Could I say in the end that it was worth the wait? What's more, could I say that this unique journey of my life was worth it? The upcoming kiss was only one small symbol of the life I had chosen … the life I had been given. Everyone was going to see the first kiss, but they all had no idea of the journey leading there. The journey of my life.

The Journey's Beginning

This book is the story of my journey down the unbroken road. I am here to tell you my story and how I arrived to where I am now.

You will read about a little, freckled girl raised in the Blue Ridge Mountains of North Carolina. A child who was raised by her mama, taught by her daddy and guided in the path of the Truth, though she wavered from it time after time. This story swells with scents of honeysuckles and African earth. It's background is the music of orchestras and the cries of babies born and unborn. It rolls with images of lonely tears and joyful celebrations.

These are the lessons of my life. This is the testimony of my deepest heart. This is an unusual narrative of a girl who saved her heart for love and grew up knowing that being unique is a gift. The pages ahead are filled with the rawest images of my soul, the good and the bad.

One may wonder why would I write all of this down. Why would I let these words be read? I have only one answer: that the story of my journey might guide someone to the One who wrote it. This book isn't like many. This one is meant to be different. I pray that it leaves a legacy … because I didn't write my story, God did. May it touch your heart.

On A Fair Spring Day

With a shrill scream, I made my entry into the world. Swaddled in a soft blanket, my father proclaimed my name to a throng of thrilled family and friends.

My grandmothers began to cry at the sound of their names: Kathryn, for my daddy's mother and Mary for my mama's mother. They each held me and whispered sweet words in my tiny ears.

The nineteenth day of April, that fair spring, was beautiful. With the dogwood trees blooming and the promise of summer in the air, my pretty mama and handsome daddy took me home. Daddy laid me gently in the basinet, feeling the weight of the world on his shoulders. He breathed deeply with responsibility.

Little did I know that I had been born into such a precious family. I didn't know my needs, but Kevin and Pam Brown did and they never gave up. I relied on my parents and they raised me. Thus begins my story.

2

FEAR TO FREEDOM

Earliest Memories

S now falling softly. Mama and Daddy's voices talking gently to one another in the living room after my bedtime. Birthday candles. Church bulletins covered in childish scribbles. Rolling down the hallway of our little house.

These were the sounds, sights and smells of my earliest memories.

Then came Kandace. Kandace was born when I was three and a half. She was a round-faced doll baby. Her personality was clearly visible from the start. We were best friends. I was the compliant, easy one and Kandace was the mischievous little one. We were a pair.

Mama and Daddy decided to homeschool us. It was a little revolutionary. God planted the idea in my mom's heart first. She didn't want to have to leave Kandace and me to go off to work. When looking in the Bible for what to do about our education, she didn't find anything about public school systems; nothing about the government being responsible for everything the children are taught. So, they decided that there seemed to be a "good," "better" and "best" in regard to where children receive their education. They felt the best option was teaching their own children.

My cousins, Taylor and Leah, were also homeschooled by their mom, my daddy's sister. My Aunt Kim and Mama joined together and taught the four of us. Taylor and I loved learning together. Both of our mothers were fabulous teachers and taught us more than we could have ever received anywhere else.

After a few years, our moms decided to go their separate ways and do school separately. I missed Taylor, but I still enjoyed home-schooling. Sometimes other people didn't understand why we did what we did, but Mama and Daddy would just say, "It's okay to be different as long as it is a good different. It makes us stronger."

My early childhood was simple and carefree. Then I began encountering an evil adversary that seemed to make his presence known at my most vulnerable time ... nighttime. My struggle would be one that would last for some time.

Not Against Flesh and Blood

My arched window allowed the moon to send a bluish glow over my bed. The only sound I could hear was the hum of the fan in the hallway. My sheets were pulled up to my chin and I laid flat on my back.

I knew it was coming. I could feel it like a shadow over me, enveloping me. It seeped into my very flesh until I shook. My clock's red glow said:

1:16 a.m.

Why again?

I gripped at my pillow. I wanted to get up. I wanted to run to Daddy and Mama. I had to get to them, but it held me back. I flung my body over, trying to think of something else. My room's contents were barely visible in the faint light. My cozy, purple room and the elegantly high ceiling above with cute stuffed animals all around. A perfect little girl's room. Certainly not the place for what was consuming me. It belonged in some unsafe shack somewhere. Not here, not with me.

It came nonetheless. The quiet shattered into a roaring. It sounded like rushing water ... or like so many voices I couldn't distinguish one of them from another. I tried to cover my ears, yet the sounds were in my ears, or maybe it was deep in my head.

Fear.

It wracked my body. It was so thick in the air I could have grabbed it. I wish I could have grabbed it and killed it like a deadly living beast, but it was not physical. It could not be touched.

My thoughts went wild. Above the roar came one voice louder than all of the others. It was icy. The familiar voice.

This will never end.

I was too afraid to cry. I had no proper weapons to battle this voice, so it continued.

Everyone will die. You will be alone. Forever alone.

I wrung my sheets in my clammy hands.

Every night I will haunt you. You will sleep for only moments at a time. You will be exhausted always.

I whimpered in terror. It mocked me.

What is wrong with you?! That is what everyone will ask. They don't know how dark this is. They won't know how real this is. And this is so real, isn't it? You come from a wonderful family. You have no right to feel this way. This shouldn't be a problem you face. And that is why I am here.

I closed my eyes.

Stop trying to sleep! You won't. I will use anything to keep you awake, to terrify you.

The voice was all that remained.

I am not leaving. Worry will haunt you forever. Fear will be your enemy. I will be your worst nightmare. Forever.

I finally dozed off from pure exhaustion.

Throughout the day, the fear would stay away. It seemed as though the light of day warded it off. However, when darkness came, so did it. I was not afraid of darkness. I could have wandered through a forest of blackness and never shuddered once. No, what I was afraid of was deeper than darkness.

I hated when Mama would tell me it was time for bed. Daddy and Mama both saw the tears in my eyes. After so many nights of my fear, Daddy understood.

Daddy sat at my bedside for hours. He told me that the voices were Satan's demons trying to scare me.

"They are lies, sweetheart. Don't believe them."

I found that other issues started to arise. There was the odd and strange desire to make certain that everything in my room was in perfect order before bed. My curtains had to be perfectly closed or it was possible that I could see the imaginary faces through the glass. Hours passed as I left my bed to fix something, repairing mistakes I had missed. It nearly drove me mad.

Daddy could hear my feet hitting the hardwood floor over and over hours after I should have fallen asleep.

"Lie down, Katy."

His tall frame filled the doorway.

"Daddy, I can't."

"Now." His voice was firm.

I sat down on the bed, pulling my knees to my chest. Daddy said something that made me forget my anger.

"I used to be like you. I would lay in the bed at night, afraid."

I couldn't believe it. Maybe I wasn't crazy.

"That fear didn't have to have power over me. I thought it did. I thought it would never go away. Do you know what I did?"

I looked up into his blue eyes, ready for his answer.

"I quoted Scripture."

I couldn't help but feel disappointed. That was it?

"Katy, you need to ask Jesus to save you. Satan will have no power over you then."

No. No, not that again. Why couldn't he stop talking about that? I didn't want to get "saved" as all the gray-headed preachers said. Why couldn't he understand?

"No, Daddy. Not now."

He didn't push it. "Then give Scripture a chance. Say a Bible verse when you are afraid. Fear is defenseless against it."

Daddy was handing me the sharpest weapon. It was the one I needed; yet, all I saw was a dull weapon ... one that stood weak to the challenge of my great fears. At least that's what the enemy told me.

That night the fear came and with it, one of its new tactics. It persuaded me that my sins would keep me from Heaven. I didn't need Jesus. Instead, it told me that I had to remove my sins on my own.

Your mama is mad at you.

I would rush out of my bed and into the living room.

Mama saw me. I stood there, my skinny legs trembling in the draft of the hallway.

"What is it?"

"You mad at me, Mama?"

"No. I'm not. Why do you ask?"

"No reason," I turned to leave and then turned back to face her. "I am sorry for anything I may have done wrong today, okay? If I did anything bad, I'm sorry. I didn't mean to do anything bad, but sometimes–"

"Katy. Okay. Go to bed."

I slid beneath my sheets convinced that my sins were gone. But there were always more sins that fear would uncover. I couldn't go back to Mama and Daddy and I couldn't wake up my sister. I lay there until my need for sleep won.

That was only the beginning of my fight to cleanse my own sins. My fear turned my healthy need for forgiveness from sins into a monster in my little mind. I would be convinced I had sinned in ways that I had never even imagined. It tortured me. Unlike the paranoia of making my room perfect, this was a burden that I could not control. Mama, Daddy and Kandace all told me to stop constantly asking for their forgiveness. It was not heartfelt, it was a ball and chain that I just needed to get off and so I did ... until it came back again.

But the voices. They were the worst. The voice. It was the scariest. It was the core of my fear. And true to its word, it still came. Night after night.

Lying in bed, feeling helpless one night I squeezed my eyes closed and opened my mouth.

"I waited patiently for the Lord ... He turned to me and heard my cry. He lifted me out of the slimy pit."

That won't help. You know that weapon is weak.

I didn't care. The more I talked, the quieter the voice got.

"He set my feet on a rock and gave me a firm place to stand."

No voice ... no roar. Nothing.

"Get behind me, Satan!" I sat up. Shivering with new-found strength, I went on. "Greater is He that is in me than he that is in the world!"

I fell asleep. For the first time in a long time... fear had lost.

I turned 8-years-old on April 19th 2002. In June, my church had Vacation Bible School. I dreaded it. Actually, I hated it. I didn't hate the people or the activities. I just hated the feeling it gave me. I felt like I had a war going on in my stomach, replicating the one in my mind.

It was as always. The first few days passed with games, music and Kool-Aid. Thursday came and so did "the talk." I despised every one of those "talks." I had heard enough salvation messages and speeches to lead a hundred souls to Jesus. But I had a heart of stone. Even as an 8 year old, I was almost unbending. Almost.

The teacher handed out little cards. On the card, I had several choices. I skimmed over it, wishing the moment would pass. Beside one checkbox were the words, I am a Christian. Beside another said, I am a not Christian. The last said, I am not a Christian but I would be willing to talk about it.

My hand lingered over the second choice. There was that feeling again. That was the reason I couldn't stand being there.

I checked the third box. I wasn't sure why. I just did. Before I could change my mind, the card was gone. I wished with all of my heart that no one would bother me about it.

But they did.

Standing at the top of the stairs to go to recess that afternoon, my teacher stopped me.

It began with, "Katy, can we talk?"

There it was. That dreaded moment. I plopped down on the couch beside her. She told me that she saw what I had put on my card.

I began to battle in my mind.

Here it comes again. Just ignore it like always.

I couldn't handle it this time. Was there a yelling preacher in front of me condemning me to hell? No. Was I in a life or death situation? No. Was there a huge performance going on to persuade me to salvation? No. There was nothing at all, except for the quiet lady beside me, asking me one simple question.

"Do you want to ask Jesus into your heart?"

Everything came to one monumental peak in my mind and heart. The battle was at its climax. Yet, I sat there letting it rage. If it weren't now, it would be never.

No. Don't do it.

Choose. I broke into a gush of tears.

"Yes."

"Would you like to now?"

"I just want my mama here."

That was easy. Mom was a few yards away in the music class-room. She was suddenly in front of me, on her knees.

Her voice was soothing, yet my heart battled on.

"Just pray, Katy. Ask Him."

I did. It was a weepy mass of jumbled words, but somewhere along the way I begged Jesus to save me and I believed. I truly believed.

Freedom.

Cleansing.

Joy.

I looked up to see the world through knew eyes. Not ones of fear, but rather, ones of courage and strength.

A few nights later I was in bed. The room was darker than usual.

Your room needs to be fixed. Stuff is messed up … like always.

I cringed as I refused. No. I wouldn't get up.

You have to. I control you.

Lies. I called out to Jesus.

Don't do that.

My Savior came. He gave me strength. The fear came still, yet it did not consume me. It was held at bay by my Father's arms. I spoke the Word of God.

"The Lord is my Shepherd …"

This time it meant more to me. This time I believed. My enemy retreated. It promised to come back, but this time I wasn't frightened by its promise. I knew that its fight would no longer be against me, but rather against the One who had already won the war. I was His and He was mine. With that truth, I fell into a peaceful slumber.

Rescued

Life as a little girl in the not so metropolis Wilkesboro, North Carolina was simple. Life was as sweet as the corn that grew in the backyard. My Dad worked at a company that sold wood flooring, windows, and doors. He was a professional businessman. A hard worker. He always seemed to be busy. But there was one thing I loved about his job. Vacations. They were business trips for my Dad, but for me they were certainly not that. They were fun.

A few months before I accepted Christ, there was a camper moving down the road loaded with two families, my dad's boss's family (the Churches) and mine. This would be a trip that I, nor my family, would ever forget. The Church family and mine got along quite well. They had two very young children and a son a few years older than myself.

I remember very little about the drive to Florida other than an overwhelming feeling. Nausea. I always struggled with carsickness, but this time was horrible. I had ridden nearly six hours sideways in the large camper. I felt like I was in a covered wagon. I was miserable. Daddy told me to look at the road and I would be fine. But I couldn't see the road and suddenly I was covered in vomit. Before I knew it, Mom was slinging me up towards the little trashcan.

That was only the beginning. We stayed in one of the most beautiful hotels in America. It had a little town in the middle of it. I spent so much time in the sun, though lathered in sunscreen; I still managed to turn bright red. It was one of those hot days by the pool that Kandace slipped off her float suit. She couldn't swim yet and so she always wore her yellow "floaty." The extremely large pool was buzzing with people. Mom had to really look to see where we were from her folding chair by the pool. Kandace ate a snack beside Mom and was quickly ready to jump back in the cool water. Mom was talking to someone and in one quick moment ... Kandace was gone. She was up on the long slide at the other end of the massive shimmering, blue water. She slid down and plunged into the deep water. Mom looked down to see Kandace's floaty at her feet. Panic.

"Kandace!!!"

Mom's eyes caught a glimpse of a flailing child by the slide. Adrenaline sent her into high gear and she practically leapt from her chair into the water. In a couple of seconds, Mom grasped Kandace. Her pudgy, terrified face was slipping below the surface of the water. Mom pulled her shaking frame out of the pool, holding her against her chest.

As though the trip hadn't been catastrophic enough, it would get crazier. A few days later we went to the great Disney World. Mom picked out a shiny purple shirt for me to wear. It would be a perfect day. I was thrilled. I would get to see all of the Disney Princesses. It was wonderful for the first few hours, though extraordinarily hot. We ended up by a store surrounded by identical looking flowerbeds. Daddy had to talk to someone on the cell phone, so we all went to the restroom and then sat on one of the many benches. I asked Mom if I could go into the store that was only a few feet away. She agreed and said that she would come inside in a moment. She said to stay nearby. I walked into the cool store with the sweat drying on my neck, I found a jewelry rack. There were Minnie Mouse earrings, princess necklaces and castle-themed bracelets. I had recently gotten my ears pierced, so I chose a pair of earrings. I left them hanging on the rack and went to find Mom. I looked down a couple of aisles, expecting to find Kandace and Mom around any corner. But they were nowhere to be seen, so I walked out the double glass doors. Everything looked the same. I looked around for Dad. Where were the restrooms? Everything was different, yet everything was the same. Flowerbeds.

Everywhere. The people so densely filled the area. I forced myself to think clearly.

Relax. They are around here somewhere. Just keep looking.

I looked, I searched. Panic. I felt it rising up my spine, heating me whole body.

Where are they?

It had only been a few minutes, but I felt so very alone. I began to cry.

"Have you seen my mom?"

The man I had asked shook his head, no. I asked a few more people and then I began to say it repeatedly, randomly and frantically.

"Have you seen my mommy? daddy! Have you seen my daddy?"

Flowerbeds.

Where was Kandace's stroller? Where was Daddy? How had I gotten so lost?

In the midst of my thoughts I felt a hand on my arm. Mama. I turned and saw a young woman's face. She was a brunette with a bob-cut. Average height, average weight and pretty. I couldn't see her eyes, because of her dark sunglasses. She was pushing a baby stroller and in it was a beautiful, perfect baby girl with a large pink bow in her short blond hair. Like a baby doll.

"Stay right here. Your mommy will find you," she said calmly.

Somehow, I trusted this woman. I felt safe. Maybe it was the fact that she had a baby of her own. Maybe it was the way she pulled me to her side. But regardless of the reason, I stayed. My eyes darted as I looked for a familiar face. The sun sparkled off of my shimmery, purple shirt like a beacon in the night.

"Katy!"

Mama's voice. I had never been so happy to hear my name. She pushed through the crowd with full abandon. She caught me in her arms. I hugged her. I turned to tell the nice lady "thank you." She was gone. Not a sign of her. Mom had swept me away and back in Daddy's arms. Daddy was in a cold sweat. We all were. Tears streamed down our faces. Kandace was not nearly as concerned and we all laughed when she once again asked for the t-shirt she had seen in the store. She got her shirt and I got my earrings.

I later found out that that store had two entrances … one on each side. The doors looked identical, as did the majority of the outside of both doors. I had exited through the opposite door from which I had entered. The many flowerbeds had made me disoriented. There had been so many people and I was so small that I hadn't been able to see my dad.

I don't know who that lady was. I don't know from where she came. The truth is, Dad sometimes calls her "an angel." But there is one thing I know about that woman. She saved me. People may say all day long that it is not unusual for children to get lost in Disney World. Maybe it isn't unusual, but as I stood there that day as an 8-year-old, dripping in a cold sweat, I felt as though I was the only one who had ever been so lost. If it hadn't been for that lady, I would have kept walking. I would have run further away from safety, yet, she stopped me. She kept me in the area, so that Mom could find me. To her I owe a great many thanks … or just maybe it's God I should thank, because regardless of whether she was an angel or not, she worked for God that day.

The Florida trip had its fair share of rough spots, but all in all, I had a grand time. I was less than pleased when we arrived home to what seemed a boring house, boring food and a boring life.

A Greater "Lost"

When I look back at those days and that one particular day when I had wondered if I would ever see my family again, I am reminded of God's power; I am reminded that though I was lost, I am found. I realized that in life, we are all lost. We are born looking for a purpose, a reason to live. Something that is bigger than ourselves. Some fill that need for purpose with superficial fillers. Yet, things like money, jobs, stuff and even family and friends can't fill this void. Many don't know that, so they walk around like I did in Disney World. They are alone. They are lost. Unlike me, many don't even know they are lost. They think they are going in the right direction, when in reality they are walking in circles or in the wrong direction all together. They need someone like the "angel lady" to stop them, to tell them that they are going the wrong way. They need to know that the only true life one can have comes from the One who gives life. Jesus Christ is the only way. He is the only One who can make us not lost anymore. Because He died on a battered cross 2,000 years ago and was the perfect man who took our sins upon Himself, we can be found. We can be saved. Not only saved from a worthless existence on this earth, but from an eternity in hell. There is no need to be lost. We can be found. Rescued. Redeemed.

As Daddy cradled my head against his chest that hot April day in Disney World, I was experiencing only a small portion of the way it feels to be in God's arms. I was learning there is no safer place than in the care of Almighty God. This was the greatest lesson of my life.

3
SWEET
HONEYSUCKLE
CHILDHOOD

My Oldest Friend

When I was nine and ten years old, I would pull my bicycle out of the garage. I slipped on my plastic sandals at the door and took off riding up the grassy hill. I passed by my Papaw and Mamaw's house (my Dad's parents). My young legs easily pushed against the pedals. I rode down the gravel road that connected to their driveway. The road opened into a grassy expanse and down a steep hill. I caught speed and felt like I was flying. My speed propelled me all the way to the house far to the left. The large brick house grew closer and I jumped off the bike while it slowed. I would lean it against the hand railing on the steps and knock on the door. I always knew the lock would slide and the door would open.

"Hello, Katy!"

My great-grandmother welcomed me in, like she always did. I loved her house. The scent of an old home made me feel at peace. The living room was cozy and warm. The kitchen was old-fashioned with flowers on the windowsill. The upstairs had a library with leather chairs. The cool basement was lined with shelves and shelves of canned vegetables. On holidays, the large home would nearly burst with family. The dining room's long table would be laden with food. The home brought joy to all who entered it. It was a pleasant place.

Grandma Ruth was a more amazing woman than I realized at my young age. She had gone through a lot along with her husband, C.M. who had fought in WWII. Years later, in 1985, C.M. was diagnosed with colon cancer and died within a couple months. Ruth was a strong, proper lady with pearl earrings and neat clothes. She was thin and smart and a former librarian. She had given birth to my great Aunt Norma and a few years later, had my Papaw, David, in 1948.

This particular day, that wonderful woman told me to sit. So I fell onto the old yellowish couch. She sat in the chair across from me. We talked. We talked about so many things. She took me to the kitchen and opened "The Milky Way Drawer." I filled my pockets full of chocolate candy. She gave me a quick, firm hug before I left and told me that she loved me. She told me to be careful and she stood holding the screen door open as she watched me pedal up the hill.

Sometimes a few days would pass that I didn't visit her, but never too many days passed. She had become a dear friend. She knew a lot of my thoughts, my plans and dreams. Sometimes she forgot things. Daddy said it was because she had a sickness that made her forget. Once, she even asked me who lived in the white house beside of her. I had to remind her that her daughter lived there. She would nod her head. Deep in her eyes, I saw her trying to remember.

One sunny day I knocked on her door and when she opened it, a strange expression crossed her face.

"Hey! How are you?" I asked, waiting for the awkward moment to pass. It didn't.

"Hello, child. Where are your parents?"

"They are at home," I said, confused.

She let me into her house, which suddenly felt very eerie. Grandma Ruth seemed so thin ... her clothes so loose.

"You only should stay for a little while or your parents will worry," she said, with a vacant expression on her face.

"They know I'm here, Mamaw."

She recoiled at being called that.

"Who are you?" she asked.

My heart sank.

I reminded her of who I was – of who she was. That was the first day she forgot to give me Milky Way bars. Across her face burned an expression I will never forget. It was one of wanting to remember, but not being able to. The day seemed a little cloudier as I rode away. Tears stung my eyes.

Weeks passed and one day she was moved into the nursing home. I visited her, but she rarely remembered me. I always told her who I was.

The first few days of December 2005, my daddy told me that Grandma Ruth would only live a few more days. My chest ached at the thought.

We had so much in common, Mamaw Ruth and me. My Papaw reminded me of that often. He told me, that just like his mother, I was the oldest. I had responsibility. The difference was that she had been the oldest of eleven children.

On December 10th, my daddy told Mama that Grandma Ruth had died. It was a strange feeling that overtook me, one of grief and yet comfort and peace. I stood with my family at a long distance from the casket. Her many family members were between her vacant body and me, yet somehow, I felt like the closest one to her.

Her funeral came and went. Shortly afterward, my Mama handed me a shoebox or two and a few plastic bags full of Grandma Ruth's things. They were only picked over leftovers from what others didn't want, but to me they were treasures. I chose a few things, but what I remember was a small box, pearl earrings and a pin with a rose on it.

I can't count how many times I have passed by her house, growing up near her home. A few years after her death, a family bought the house. I realized that I would never again step over that threshold.

Nothing can wash away my memory of those days that I took off on my bicycle, her smile as she welcomed me in and the scent of that old home. I wouldn't trade anything for the talks I had with my wise great-grandmother. In a world where the elderly are often forgotten, I learned that they are our precious heritage. Their hearts are still young and wrinkles and cranky bones will never fool me. I learned to cherish the elderly and to seek them for counsel and wisdom, because one day they will be gone.

My Great-Grandma Ruth became my dear friend and is now one of my favorite memories. Each time I see a Milky Way bar, I smile and think of her.

Being Little

In those days, I longed to be an intelligent young adult with responsibility. I never understood when the adults would bend down, pinch my pale freckled cheeks and whisper with a sad smile, "You enjoy being little now, sweetie." I understood the meaning behind those words later.

Being little. There was simply nothing like a spring day when the end of school was so nearby and in my young heart, so far away. I was convinced that learning my multiplication tables would be the hardest thing I'd ever do and if those weren't hard enough, my new piano music would be.

I would hurry up to finish school on such a day and stuff a corn dog down my throat so I could sit by the phone and wait to get a call from my cousins. It wouldn't be long before the two of them would be huffing up the hill between our houses and I would pull Kandace out of the house into the warm air. There were no formalities between the four of us and we would soon come to a conclusion on what we wanted to do for the afternoon. For some time, we almost always decided on a trip to the creek.

We must have been quite a sight, trotting down the hill. Taylor was the second oldest of our motley crew and to my dismay, a little less than a year younger than me. She rubbed it in those six days we were the same age. She always wore her hair in a straight, smooth ponytail and never had a worry on that pretty sun-tanned, heart-shaped face of hers. She was more than happy to be the peacemaker. Of course, my sister Kandace was the one who would be skipping with her curly brown mane blowing in the breeze. She always had herself into something and required constant attention during those days. Leah, the wee little girl, was too much like me in many ways. The little blond-headed baby of the group always helped me make the decisions and, unlike her older sister, preferred to play the cowboy in our games. Then there was me. The only one with the white, freckled skin and feet browner than my face. I would be beside Taylor skipping along; trying not to worry about something … whatever it was that particular day.

The creek always seemed to smell fresh and the water was cool, cold really. The rich green moss lined the creek's embankment like a velvety carpet for our bare feet. I always had to remind one of the younger girls to watch out for the "three shiny leaves" because that was poison ivy. We were told by our wise fathers to wade no further than our knees, but Taylor was usually the only one who remembered the unwanted advice. We were always thrilled when we found a new place that the water flowed slowly and a fallen tree provided a good seat. It wouldn't be long, however, before we grew tired of our new playing place and would go in search of a better one.

On such a day at the creek, I persuaded Leah that a sled would make an excellent boat in the deeper water. As I remember, both of our mothers had told us on that particular day, "we were not to get wet," but I explained that the sled wouldn't let a drop of water on her. She was skeptical, but being the 7-year-old that she was, she gave in. It was to Taylor's dismay. I dug through our winter sleds on that summer day and found the large black one, Old Ruth, as we would later name it. I hurried everyone down the steep path to the still waters before my poor cousin could change her mind. I lowered the plastic sled to float on the dark surface of the cold water. Leah whined, but I sternly told her that it was too late to change her mind. Taylor stood at a distance. I supposed so that when my plan failed, she wouldn't be in trouble. I helped lower Leah onto the sled and she sat there for a moment, but to my horror the hateful Old Ruth began to bow up and water rushed in over Leah as she screamed. She stood up, which just made matters worse as she slipped off the sled and catapulted under the coldness. I could hear nothing but a trio of three little girls' screams as I pulled my soaked cousin out of the water. Needless to say, I was left at the creek alone as everyone ran up the path to tattle-tale on me. As I recall, I never tried using a sled for a boat ever again.

Despite each of our strangeness and oddities, we always asked our parents for one more hour to play. And we played everywhere. The woods were our favorite place of all. Intermingled with the evergreen trees and tall oaks, we would drape old sheets from branches and create houses. We would act out stories of the Old West. We had many a series and it would take us days and even months to get through a story. We traipsed around in old dresses that we had rummaged through in the musty basements of our houses. We took play-acting seriously. Each story was produced in the deep forest as though it were a movie being filmed. Leah was usually frustrated that she had to play such girly games and would only be satisfied if she could be the cowboy or Indian and kill one of us.

And then one day she invented a game where I had to be an evil old woman who treated her as a slave. She got to go behind my back and play tricks on her mean master. Even Taylor and Kandace enjoyed that series and said I was good at being a bossy, mean mistress. I was mad at them for about a day.

I think we all got addicted to popsicles those hot summers. Some days we would even sneak inside and take turns sticking our sweaty, beet-red faces in the freezer. Before long, school started back up and we each had to spend the majority of our days in our homes. The air would lose its warmth and as the briskness of fall set in, we would be hard-pressed to give up our outside escapades despite the chill. The creek was no longer refreshing, but simply cold, so we stayed near our playhouses and were satisfied mixing dirt and flour together to create our pretend meals. We crushed acorns and ground leaves for herbs. The outside faucet was our best friend as we toted water to and from our activities at the edge of the yard. Usually, we would argue on whose turn it was to get the water, but often it ended with sweet Taylor picking up the bucket and getting it herself.

Later in the fall, the whole family headed to the beach to spend a week in a rented house by the ocean. It became a tradition somewhere along the way for the four of us girls to put on a "show" in the living room of the house for the six adults. Each year I packed half of my suitcase full of costumes, rather than swimsuits. I spent the beginning of the week planning our show. I was the director, being the "show lady" I was, and spent the whole week begging Leah to be a part of my masterpiece. One particular year, out of the kindness of her heart, she agreed to be in my show. I had chosen to base my masterpiece on *The Sound of Music*. We each acted out one of the children in the movie and sang several of the songs. I had never been so thrilled in my life when the six adults gave a thunderous applause, which I believed was heartfelt. Later, Kandace whispered in my ear, "We will never do that again." But for me, it didn't matter. I had performed my show.

The first snow was always a cause for celebration … even if it was only half an inch. We pulled out our sleds, though not to drown Leah in the creek this time, but to use them to actually sled. After wrapping up in warm clothes, we braced ourselves for the chill of the white world outside. We would head back inside after climbing the sledding hill more times than we could count, with our thighs burning, our socks in a wad at the toe of our boots and chapped cheeks. As soon as we entered the enveloping warmth, we began to figure out how we could get everyone on the hill, including our two grandparents, to eat supper together. After much difficult planning, Kandace usually came to our daddy with the question, since he couldn't seem resist his cute, youngest daughter. Before long, he was calling my aunt and grandparents. Meanwhile, we were in the pantry persuading my mother that we did indeed have the ingredients to make chili. As the night fell, we trudged up the snow-laden hill to the home of my Mamaw and Papaw. We sat around the dinning room table eating crackers and chili as happy as larks. With full stomachs, we marched down the hall to Mamaw and Papaw's king-size bed and watched a movie and played a board game. We would relax in the comfort and warmth of our family's presence. How sweet it was!

Things changed over the years, as we grew up. Conversations between our crew changed as well. No longer were we calling each other about who would bring the sheets for our tents. We ceased mixing flour and water or searching for a new place to play at the creek. We no longer played out our stories or dressed in costumes. I would not trade anything for those days, because I now realize those were some of the most precious days that made me who I am. Those were the days in which we were safely cared for. We were taught and loved. We were allowed to be children. Innocent children. I never would have imagined those days would have disappeared so quickly. At the time it seemed that they would always be there. The creek hasn't changed, the playhouse still sits where it always has, but life moved on. There was a time for freckles, popsicles, and sleds for boats. A time for bicycle rides to Grandma's house, simply time for being a child. There is also a time to remember those memories as we walk on in our adult lives. The miles have separated us, yet when I go to my childhood home, I sometimes stop and walk outside to the playhouse. If I stand there for a little while, I can almost see four little girls playing and simply enjoying being little.

Exploring My Talents

I became a lover of music and art in my childhood. My mama was impressed by my ability to draw and paint. One day, I began art lessons. The first few months, I battled my clinging fear of doing anything alone. Feeling the paintbrush stroke the canvas brought me pleasure. Over time I grew out of having to have Mama nearby all of the time.

One day, we were riding in the van when Daddy turned the radio station to the classical station. Every once in a while he wanted Kandace and me to listen to classical music. He said that it broadened our minds. The piece playing was a riveting piano solo. I listened in wonder. Daddy turned his head slightly so his voice would easily meet my ears.

"Isn't that beautiful? Would you like to play the piano? One day you could play like that."

I didn't answer. I doubted that I could ever play anything as awe-inspiring even if I practiced forever. Piano lessons began when I was eight years old. My piano teacher, Ms. Becky was pleasantly surprised at my ability to play chords and scales with ease. I wasn't the quickest of learners, but I tried hard. One of my greatest fears was to embarrass myself in front of my teacher. At Christmastime, Mama scheduled me to play at church. I begged her not to make me play. Her big brown eyes turned cool.

"Katy, you will never overcome your fear until you face it."

I was dressed in a velvet dress and my straight hair was brushed until it shined. I shook with nervousness as I opened my piano book and sat on the squeaky bench. I played "Mary, Did You Know?" I did well. Everyone clapped and I swelled with pride. Maybe Mama was right. Many other little girls and boys took piano lessons, but their mommies never made them play in church. They told Mama that their child was just too afraid. My Daddy and Mama always told me that parents who let their children succumb to fear of performing ultimately teach their children that there is indeed something to fear. At the moment, with my little knees shaking together, I was frustrated with my parents for insisting I play, but when it was all over – even when years had passed – I was grateful that they had pushed me. Whether it is in music, athletics, public speaking or any other number of activities, I learned that practice was important, but performing was just as important. Performing in front of a crowd of loud fans or a silent audience develops a whole new and unchartered territory of the brain. Yet, for me, it brought a grin to my face and inspiration to my heart which I would have never known otherwise.

Innocence

The years passed and I entered a busier, technological age. I felt like we lost the beautiful simplicity of being young and innocent. I learned that just maybe outside is still the greatest playground. And Mama's old sheets still make wonderful tents in the woods. I benefited from my parents letting nature teach me. I only wished that other children could have been shielded from the carnal and secular world-view that was so ready to seep into their hearts.

My mom and dad protected me, but they didn't put me in a bubble. They let me grow up without the pressure of the world caving in around me. I saw that there is a time in a child's life when their will, courage, and passion for God should be cultivated. When a child is taught and trained in the home, parents have massive and extensive time and opportunity to teach him, like my parents did for me. It was clear, just teaching children math, reading and science wasn't enough; the Bible is the most important part and it is the part that schools are banned from teaching.

I grew up in a "greenhouse" of sorts. I don't know a lot about plants, but I do know that you can't take a tender, young plant and plant it in the raw outside ground and hope it survives the scorching sun and cold nights. The elements are too strong and too hard. The plant has a much better chance at growing if it is in a greenhouse. It is sheltered from the overpowering sun and drenching rains there. It can grow in safety and then one day it will be ready for the tough world outside.

I learned from parents, who knew far more than I, that children need a greenhouse. Why would so many parents think that their 3-year-old could be a missionary in preschool? It would only be a short period of time before he would turn to the worldliness that surrounds him. Just because a child was born into a Christian family, doesn't mean that he will automatically be able to lead the masses to Jesus. Most young children will whither in the pressures of the world and if they do survive the pressure, that is a blessing for sure, but I wondered, why chance it? Why hope that they make it in a culture where they are blasted with false information that is totally against Scripture? Why not show them the truth, when that knowledge will forever impact their lives, so when they do leave the home, they will be ready and prepared?

I was blessed to be one of those children who could grow in the Truth before exposure to the icy lies of the world. I was not brainwashed or kept from thinking for myself. I was pushed to explore and learn and choose for myself the path I would follow. Yet, I saw the outside. I watched other children suffer through the brash and crude "real world" that their parents were always telling me I needed to join. I tucked away in my heart the desire to tell anyone I found that the best place for a child to be is in the protection of his or her loving parents. If a child didn't have parents to care for him, then someone who would be like a parent to him, could train him. What a pleasure it was to be held close with my passion for God nurtured. I waited patiently knowing that when it was time for me to fly, I would be able to soar.

4
THE CHINA DOLL

The Orphan

One of many.

The baby in the rusty crib was just one of many in the gray room. The baby girl was an orphan and her only home was this place called an orphanage in one of China's many cities. Her little belly rumbled with hunger and tears trickled down her cheeks. She knew better than to cry aloud. Though she was only several months old, she knew that crying didn't change anything. She waited. In the crib beside her laid another baby girl and beside her laid another. On they went down the length of the dingy room. All babies with different mother and fathers. All babies that had been given up. All were left there for different reasons. Where they came from mattered little now. They were in need of love and of hope.

Thunk.

One of the few ladies that worked there had dropped a bottle into the baby's crib. It was a little too far out of the wee girl's reach, but no one was there to help her or hold her. She rolled over and grasped at the bottle. Finally, holding it to her lips, her tears dried. Her diaper was full and her skin was grimy, but there were too many babies to give them all proper care. The women worked all day and night to care for the babies, yet they only scratched at the surface of their needs.

The many little girls lining the room needed more than an occasional bottle. They needed a family. They needed a mother to rub their hair and kiss their cheeks and say, "I love you." But in their homeland, there was no room for them. Most had been left on the steps of the building because they were not what the family wanted... or needed. And since families in China were only permitted to have one child, many wanted a healthy boy to carry on the family name and protect the couple in their old age. To many, a girl was unwanted and unnecessary. And if there were ever any health problems, the baby was even more unwanted. Yet, that never stopped many of the Asian mothers from softly sobbing as they were forced to lay their daughters on the hard steps of the orphanages.

The Dream

I was standing in front of my family's swing-set behind the house. I was pushing a small child on the plastic swing. Back and forth. I realized that I had never seen this child before. I looked down at her face as the swing brought her up towards me. She was an adorable, little Asian girl with dark, almond-shaped eyes and olive-colored skin. She was no more than two- or three-years-old. She was precious and beautiful. She was my sister. Somehow I was convinced that she was a part of my family. We had adopted her. I didn't even know her, but I loved her.

I woke up.

It was all a dream, but it was so real. I placed my feet on the floor of my bedroom that day in 2004. I was the ripe old age of ten. I breathed deeply and closed my eyes as the face of the little girl already had begun to fade.

Now, I am not the kind of person that thinks all of my dreams are a sign of some sort. I didn't even believe that this one was a sign. But regardless, it helped begin a new chapter of my life and of my family's. This dream didn't seem like the kind of dream that came and then flittered away with the day's activities. This one seemed to remain with a purpose.

That night, Daddy and Mama prayed with Kandace and me before we went to sleep in our bedrooms. Once we had finished, Mama went ahead to go to the living room. Dad stayed in my room for a while longer, sitting on the edge of my bed as I shared the dream.

I wasn't planning on sharing the dream with him, but lying there with him sitting on the side of my bed, I just felt a prompting to tell him. I was afraid that he would laugh and say, "What is that supposed to mean?" or "That was just a dream."

"Daddy, I had a dream last night. And it was so real. It almost felt like – don't think I am crazy – but a sign of some sort."

"What was it?" he asked.

As I told him, his face changed. I glimpsed the faintest shimmer of tears in his blue eyes. He stood up abruptly and walked into the hallway.

"Pam! Can you come here for a minute?"

I was surprised. What was so special about my dream? Mama quickly walked into my bedroom. Dad spoke slowly and with a shaky voice, "Now, Katy, tell your mom what you told me."

I told her what I had shared moments before. Her face changed as well as I got to the part about the Asian girl. I said that I was pretty convinced that she was Chinese. I claimed that it was one of those dreams … the kind that God uses to tell you something. Daddy looked up at Mama. Mom's mouth literally hung open. I wanted to say, "What is it?" but in a way I knew. They must have already known something of this. Maybe there was something I needed to know.

Daddy didn't really explain. He just looked up at Mama and said, "Can you believe that?" Mama just shook her head from side to side.

It was only a short time later when Daddy explained what had shocked them so. They had been praying about adoption for some time. Adoption from China. They had just returned from an Adoption Conference with America World Adoption. I hadn't known where my parents were going the night they had gone to hear more about international adoption. I had stayed with my grandparents and had assumed it was something to do with Dad's work. But little did I know that they had been praying and considering adoption. My dream was just another way of confirming it. God was speaking to all of us.

It became official and we began the adoption process. We shared the news with everyone and all were thrilled. Dad and Mama were quickly bombarded with extensive paperwork. A nice social worker came to our house. It was a long, slow process for my family. For me, it was a matter of knowing that I had to be the sister this little girl needed. For my parents, it was a myriad of responsibilities. Late into the night, my parents studied and filled out stacks of paperwork. Countless warm sheets of paper came off the weary printer.

We were riding in the van to town one day when Mama broke the silence.

"What do you girls think about the name Clara?"

"Katy, Kandace and Clara," Kandace chirped. "It's great!"

The First Clara

Travel back to 1950 to a house bustling with eight children. A woman not even five feet tall stands at the sink washing a pile of dishes. Her name is Clara. Her life is not an easy one. She is married to a busy and tough man named Frank. She has a passel of eight children to tend to. A lot is required of her and she doesn't have much to her own name, except relentless love and patience. But if one was standing in the doorway to this little woman's kitchen they could hear her. She isn't singing. She is talking. Though there isn't a soul in the room, she speaks. A person might say that she is crazy, but they would be wrong. She talks to her Father. Sometimes tears trickle down her weathered cheeks as she talks. She is praying. She leans on her Heavenly Father's loving arms because she needs love. And because she gleaned her love from her Maker, she shows love to all who know her. Her life doesn't hold much. There is a lot of hard work and many tiresome days. Yet, she smiles.

Her youngest daughter was born in May of 1948. The baby girl was named Kathryn. Clara held her close and never realized that her baby's name would become my namesake. Kathryn. She and Frank nicknamed the baby girl, Kathy.

This sweet woman loved her babies and worked with all of her heart as she raised them in the misty foothills of North Carolina's Blue Ridge Mountains. She sacrificed and suffered so that her children would have all they needed. One night, she hung a pretty dress she had just finished sewing for Kathy on the curtain rod of the living room. It was a rare thing to have a new dress and little Kathy would get to wear it for the first time the following morning to school. Clara had used her precious sewing machine and had stitched each seam with care, as she had for her other seven children's clothing. Money was too tight for store-bought clothes.

This night, turmoil knocked at their door. In her chilly home on that cold evening, the stovepipe caught the upper room, where some of the boys slept, on fire. The wooden home took mere minutes to become consumed. The whole family ran outside and watched as the house burned. Clara saw the dress hanging on the curtain and snatched it up as she darted out the door. She realized that she might have a moment long enough to save her precious sewing machine before the house gave in. To her panicked mind, it seemed worth the chance of being burned or killed. She dashed for the door, but Frank grabbed her and held her back. She sobbed as her home turned to ashes.

The children were all sent to live in separate homes for a time. Eventually everyone was happily back together and all the children piled blankets in the cold parlor floor before the warming fireplace in a house they rented. This faithful lady built her home again.

Years later, in the late 1970s, she could be found taking care of my Daddy and Aunt Kim after they rode the school bus to her home each day. She would give them a hug as they hopped down from the bus and would fix them each a mayonnaise sandwich and a glass of grape Kool-Aid. Up until her death, years later, she could still be found in the kitchen talking. Talking to her Maker, because she knew that He was all she needed and sometimes, He was all she had had. Annie Clara McNiel made a lasting impression on her children and on her grandchildren. That impression stayed with my father and when it was time to name his third daughter … he remembered her.

"Clara" it would be. The beautiful name would live on.

The Picture

I was ready for a picture. I wanted to see the girl's face. I wanted to have a real, living person to look at and pray for. Eventually, Mom told Kandace and me that we would be receiving a referral soon. "Referral day" is the day all adoptive families wait and long for. It is the day when the mailman comes to the door and hands you a packet and in that packet is your baby's face. A little picture and bundle of information that will send your heart and dreams skyrocketing. Mama said that day was almost here. It was 2006 after all. I felt like it had been an eternity since my dream. I was almost 12-years-old.

January 25, 2006 we received a call from America World that we had a referral coming. The 10-month-old baby girl's name was Fu Mei Xue. I was thrilled. We had already determined that we would use her Chinese name for her middle name. My little sister's name would officially be Clara Fu Mei Brown.

The following day, as I studied a textbook in my room, I heard Mama squeal.

"Girls! Clara's picture just came in an e-mail! Come see!"

Kandace and I burst out of our rooms simultaneously. On the computer screen was a little pudgy face. A precious little face. She was adorable. She was so bundled in coats and huge pants that we couldn't really see anything but her little, round face. A few hours later, the referral came in the mail. We jumped and laughed as we held and treasured that small photo.

I recorded in my journal a couple months later:

March 3, 2006
Yeah! We have gotten the real date we will leave for China! We will leave the 22nd of March and fly out on the 23rd!

The packing began. Mama dragged out the suitcases and they slowly began to fill up over those March days. As they filled, so did my heart's excitement. We arrived in Greensboro, North Carolina the day before our plane would take off. The thrill of the adventure vanished at 2:30 a.m. on the morning of March 23rd as Daddy's voice snapped, "Girls, this is your last warning. Get up!"

I propped my eyelids opened and bundled up in sweat suit to head for the airport. When we arrived, the place looked deserted. But our plane left as the sun was beginning to turn the dark horizon into a faint purple. We landed in Michigan for a two hour layover. Kandace and I were less than thrilled with the wait, but eventually we were in the air again. If I thought that the airport had been boring, the first long flight I had ever experienced would be a shock ... and it was. We were in the air for 13 hours and at a little over eight hours until we would land, I looked over at Dad and whispered, "I'm going to lose my mind."

Then we landed in Tokyo, Japan for a very quick flight change. My only memories of Japan were greasy TV screens in the airport displaying sumo-wrestling matches. I felt sick. I was surprisingly ready to board our last flight ... for a few days at least.

Beijing. A city of over eight million people. I quickly came to term it as, "the city with no grass." It was amazing and all the same. A large bus picked us up at the airport along with several other families who were adopting. The city appeared to be never-ending, yet somehow we ended up in a large and lovely hotel somewhere in the middle of it all.

Looking out the large window from the hotel, I could see nothing but people, buildings and roads. Beijing stretched out as far as the eye could see. After such a long trip, I fell happily into the bed. I quickly learned that beds in China are not soft and plump like American beds are. Chinese beds feel like a large slab of concrete with a blanket tossed over it. Yet, when one is tired ... the softness of the bed doesn't really matter so much.

The following day, my family and 24 other families, loaded onto the large bus again to go sight-see. Each family was assigned a number that they would answer to when called. My family was number 22. The little lady at the front of the bus called out the numbers that morning.

"Family 22?" Her broken accent rang through the bus.

We raised our hands.

"Very good! Family 23?"

Off we went. Our day in Beijing was jam-packed full of visits to museums and factories. We watched silk being made, jade being chiseled and pearls being strung on string. I glanced at ancient pottery sitting in glass cases. All of the glittery silk, jade and pearls faded in comparison to one of the World's Wonders. The bus stopped along The Great Wall. Every mental imagine I had of this massive wall, were crumbled and gone at the sight of the real thing. My family and I walked the uneven steps until our legs trembled. Daddy walked further so he could see more of the gorgeous view. And it was a breathtaking view.

As amazing as The Great Wall had been, we were ready to meet Clara. I was ready to hold my sister. My parents had forewarned Kandace and me that Clara could have many mental and emotional issues. We were told that more than likely, Clara had spent the majority of her days with women. It was even possible that she had never seen a man. With all of that in mind, I was ready for whatever this child should bring with her. My family had no idea what the next day would hold as we boarded a plane to fly to Clara's hometown in the Hubei Province.

It was an exotically, green place compared to the smog of Beijing. We dragged our bags into our room and waited. In just a few hours, they would hand Clara to Mama and she would forever be ours.

After lunch we took the short walk down to the meeting hall on the fourth floor of the hotel. The room was large and needed to be after 24 families packed into the space. There was an electrical vibe of excitement and anxiousness pulsing through that room. The soon-to-be new mothers rung their hands and glanced constantly at the door in the back of the room. Behind that wall were 24 baby girls. The Chinese guides called them the "spicy girls" because most of them had very spicy and unique personalities.

A long table sat at the front of the room. Several men and women in business attire sat there with paperwork. I didn't understand it all. It seemed so confusing and complicated. I just wanted them to bring in the babies. We waited. Mom handed me the camcorder and told me to record it all. Dad and Mom were almost completely silent. We all stood along the wall as one of the guides stood up and proclaimed that the babies would start coming in and once the family's number was called, they needed to come get their baby. And so it began with the 21 families before us. Through the door came one beautiful baby after another. The families gasped with joy and the mothers tearfully held their new babies.

Family 19. Family 20. Family 21.

Mama gasped. "I see her!"

On the camcorder screen, I saw her. The most red-faced, adorable baby in a yellow and orange outfit was on the hip of one of the nannies. Little Fu Mei Xue. Though hardly little … I immediately realized that she must have been the biggest baby that had come through the door. And she was almost ours. She was seconds away from our arms.

"Family 22!"

My whole family walked to the front of the room, where the little lady handed Clara to Mom. Fu Mei had finally reached home and unconditional love. Tears ran down our faces as we walked to the back of the room. Fu Mei was in some sort of shock and looked around for a familiar face. Finding none, her little mouth opened and she began to wail. After a while, we went upstairs to our hotel room. Daddy gently told us that Clara would cry less once she felt more comfortable, but Daddy was wrong. We would need to be strong, because what our little family would face in the coming hours and days would take great strength. Fu Mei had been given up one too many times … and she was not happy about it.

Come What May

All the babies cried for the first few minutes. We had been told that they would take some time to adjust. We were prepared. Just not prepared enough. For the first few hours, we didn't even know what Clara looked like without her mouth open, face red and tears pouring down her cheeks. She screamed.

We played with her and talked to her, but nothing helped. Finally, we decided to leave the hotel room and go eat in the restaurant downstairs. Within moments of leaving the room, Clara quieted down. She looked with wide eyes at all that we passed. We sat down at the restaurant, nervous that she might start screaming again. She seemed at peace on Daddy's lap. She sat there … or was propped up there. Clara had a small amount of muscle and couldn't do physical things that most 1-year-olds can do. But she seemed calm, although sober, while we ate.

"Clara, would you like some food?"

Daddy lifted a spoonful of warm soupy-rice called congee, to her lips. She lifted her hand as Dad tried to put it in her mouth. She pushed away the food.

"Well, I'll take that as a 'no,'" Dad laughed.

A few minutes later, he tried again. She held her hand out, like an intersection traffic cop stopping traffic. Dad just kept the spoon in front of her face and after a moment, she lowered her hand. It was hilarious. She was showing who was in charge. She just sat there, stone-faced, as she gummed her food. She would occasionally drop her pudgy, little hand and let us give her a bite. The nannies had named Clara right. She was a "spicy girl."

And she was terrified. The restaurant may have been a place of an odd sort or solitude for Clara, but there were not many other places where she was happy. We walked back up to our room and within moments, she was wailing. She cried until she fell asleep. It was nice to have some quiet, even if it was just for a little while.

Mom peeked in the adjoining room where Kandace and I stayed.

"Girls, your Daddy and I have to go downstairs and sign some adoption papers. I am leaving Clara here since she is sleeping so well. She shouldn't wake up until we get back."

That seemed simple. We just needed to be quiet and all would be fine. Mom and Dad left and Kandace and I quietly watched TV and hung out. Everything was going well. It was easy as pie.

"Did you hear that?" Kandace shot up from reclining on the hotel bed.

I didn't have to wait to hear. A shrill, gurgling scream resounded from the other room. I moaned. Kandace huffed accusations at Mom and Dad for telling us that she would stay asleep. But it didn't matter now, she was awake and so I opened the adjoining door to see her in the crib. Her face was red and her clenched fists swung around in fury. I picked her up and held her close. I bounced her and dangled toys before her face. Nothing helped.

Kandace pinched her nose and demanded, as though all of this was my fault, "What is that awful smell?"

"I don't know!" I yelled over Clara.

It became obvious very soon and I was left to try to change Clara's diaper. There was no changing table, so I laid her on the clean, white bedspread and went to work. It was a disaster. I felt tears burning my eyes. I tried to remain calm, but Clara continued to wail. The mess was huge … a blowout. Kandace, being young and afraid, began to cry and begged me to let her go find Mama and Dad. I yelled "no" as she started to open the door to leave. I had two hysterical girls on my hands and I felt like I would soon become the third.

I finally had Clara clean and placed a diaper on her as well as I could. Kandace leaned against the wall, trying to calm herself and I continued trying to calm Clara. Just as I was about to go find my parents, the door clicked and they entered.

Mom looked around at the mess and wailing children and proclaimed, "What happened?"

Kandace ran into her arms in an exaggerated embrace and cried, "We almost DIED!"

A Desperate Plea for Love

I wondered if Clara would ever stop crying. Twenty-four hours after holding my sister for the first time, she was still very upset. Seeing the other little girls at the breakfast buffet with their families laughing and giggling left me confused and upset. Not because those babies were happy, but because Clara wasn't. What was even more odd was the fact that she took to Daddy more than anyone. She was generally calm while my tall, bald father held her, though at night she cried in his arms until Mama had to take her. And as soon as she felt Mama's arms, her soft sobs escalated. Clara even bit Dad's shoulder. She wasn't mean, just so afraid and angry. Before bedtime, she cried the hardest, loudest and longest.

One night I heard Kandace in the bathroom. She was crying. I could barely hear her over Clara's screams in Mom and Dad's adjoining room. I softly knocked on the bathroom door. I thought that she would tell me to go away, but she didn't.

"Come in," was her weepy reply.

I walked in to see my little sister sitting on the side of the tub in her little silky pajamas crying. Her curly hair was a mass of tangles. She was so pitiful. Her big brown, red-rimmed eyes looked up.

"Katy, is she going to be like this forever?"

I wanted to be strong. I wanted to tell her that everything would all be okay. But I didn't know.

"I don't think so. I hope not," I said.

I sat with her. I let my own tears fall. In that small bathroom in China, we were just two little foreign girls crying and praying for our sister. Our sister who was terrified and afraid. We felt like all we had in the world was one another and so we turned to each other.

Not all of those first days were hard. There were times when we would sit Clara on one of the beds in the hotel room and give her toys and for a few minutes she would be calm. We saw her smile as she played with her stack cups and held her stuffed animals. She looked up into our eyes and smiled until her almond-shaped eyes would disappear. We spent a lot of time in the bus with the other families. There was an occasional cry from the other babies, but Clara was constant. Everything upset her, it seemed. She needed routine and there was none.

We visited a village of sorts in the rural countryside of Hubei Province. The homes were unlike anything I had seen. Clara had been a foster child for a while and had lived in a home much like the ones we were visiting. It made me hold Clara even closer. Dogs pilfered through the food in the grimy corners, supposedly their kitchens. The floor was dirt and the beds were just sacks of beans and grain with rough blankets over them. Dead birds dangled from the ceiling. Outside the walls of the houses, there were miles of rice fields. This had been Clara's home. Not anymore.

As we flew to our last stop in Guangzhou, Mama and Daddy were as strong as steel. Yet sometimes their faces showed a flicker of pain as she cried, or worry as she refused to calm down. But, they showed me in their actions that they were committed totally, come what may. They showed me how they loved Clara as much as they loved Kandace or me. This baby didn't know how much she needed my mom and dad and that was why it didn't matter what happened or what was wrong; Fu Mei was Clara and her last name was the same as mine.

Finally, it was time to go home. Mom put a birthday shirt on Clara since her first birthday would pass while we were flying home. April 4th, we said goodbye to the other families that we had become friends with and flew from China to Japan. From Japan we had a 13-hour flight to Minnesota. If there had ever been a hard experience with my new sister, that flight would have been it. Clara despised flying … or so it seemed. She only wanted Dad and she only wanted my Dad to stand up and walk around as he held her.

"Sir, you must sit down."

Daddy turned to the male flight attendant. It was the third time this same man had asked him to sit down during turbulence. The plane made a small drop in the sky. There were still a few hours until the plane would land. Daddy breathed deeply as he walked back to his seat. He gritted his teeth as he slid down onto his chair, praying that Clara wouldn't notice that he was no longer walking. Her closed eyes popped open and she let out a deafening squall. A lady sitting a few feet away grabbed the male flight attendant by arm.

"Please," her voice rang out, "let the man stand up."

But the attendant didn't change his mind until the seat belt sign flickered off. And so Clara continued to cry. I almost shouted "Hallelujah!" when the plane's wheels hit the runway.

We had survived the long two days of travel when we pulled into the garage. After bringing in all of the luggage, we quickly determined that we weren't tired … or at least we didn't feel the exhaustion that was surely present. Mama and Daddy didn't make us go to bed – even though it was well past midnight. They made it very clear that this particular day was an exception to the general rule.

Clara loved home at first glance. It was wonderful to be away from strangers' constant glares at her crying. It was good to be home. Yet, my precious little sister struggled. I laid in my bed for many nights after we brought her home, listening to her cry. When I thought that she couldn't possibly have any more voice; she would let loose a blood-curdling scream. Mom and Dad held her and rocked her, but eventually they had to put her in the crib. She had to learn to go to sleep. She didn't like that.

One night, I heard a *KA–THUNK*. I jumped a foot out of my bed. It sounded like Clara had fallen out of her crib. Daddy's low voice moved across the living room. I ran down the stairs and joined them in the hallway where Clara was running toward my parents. She had jumped out of the crib. Daddy scooped her up and carried her to her room. Dad was talking to Clara and then I heard his voice change into a prayer. He prayed with his hand on her head. He begged God to give Clara peace.

It was overwhelming at times. Dad told Kandace and me that Clara had many things in her past. We had no idea the things that her parents could have been involved in. Possible generations of idol worship, paganism, alcohol and drugs could have been a part of her family's lifestyle. All of those things could have affected the way our new sister acted.

We prayed for sweet Clara and we loved on her. We kissed her little round face, dressed her up in frilly clothes, painted her little fingernails and told her every day, "We love you." Slowly, Clara believed us. Maybe it was the prayers, or the kisses, or the soft, calming words. Or all of those things together.

Years later we would joke and chuckle on how those first days with Clara had been long, tiring and unusually hard. But those days created a bond within my family. We worked through those weeks like a family should. They were so difficult that no one except Daddy, Mama, Kandace and me could understand all that happened and how God had brought us through and made Clara a child of joy, peace and love.

5

A Heart Nearly Lost

Consumed

I was sitting in the choir beside my mama when I saw him walk in the back door of the church. He was about 17-years-old and so very handsome. His blond hair stood out in the congregation as he slid into a pew. My eyes must have been glued to him all service long.

When Josh Isaacs stepped into my life that day, a new chapter of my life began … a chapter I could have lived without, or perhaps I could have handled it differently. Yet, I was 11-years-old and didn't understand or realize that what many around me considered "innocent, childhood love" could turn into something much stronger and dangerous.

A few months later, it was the summer of 2006. I would claim that it would be the most wonderful summer I had ever experienced. My life was exciting. I had a new sister. My little China doll, Clara, was finally adjusting to life in our family, and it wouldn't be long before we would adopt my little brother, Andrew. My dad had taken the roll as the Associate Pastor at the church. As for me, I was 12-years-old. I was ready to take on the world … or at least my corner of it.

I was more than thrilled about the summer, mostly because I would see one particular person very often throughout the following few months. In June, the church held a youth camp. The building was bursting with teenagers of all backgrounds and personalities. I was the young pastor's daughter. I was the so very innocent one. Most of the energetic teenagers simply ignored me. Yet, I was all right with that and knew that I was young.

I learned that though others ignored me at a young age, I never wanted to ignore others. I promised myself that when I was an older teenager, I wouldn't act like most. I wanted to be different. I wanted to be the one the younger ones looked to and said, "I can follow her." I wanted them to feel free to give me a hug and lean on me for support. Teenagers don't have to be worthless. After all, 1 Timothy 4:12 says that the young people are to "set the example" in speech, conduct, love, faith and in purity. And that was what I sought. I wanted to be an example.

I had very little of that in mind when the week began with the group riding bicycles down a mountain trail in Virginia. I fell well behind the majority of the group. Josh hung up with the wild riders … the guys. The 17-mile ride ended and we went to the river near our sleeping accommodations for the night.

Our sleeping accommodations were rustic to put it nicely. It was an old barn. Within mere moments, the guys were jumping off of a huge rock, into the churning river waters below. They screamed how the water was cold. Their lips turned blue and their faces went white. A few of the girls jumped in. Apparently, the water pulled each person down with the current to the bottom of the river. Eventually, as one's breath was almost gone, it would shoot one back to the top of the water.

"Come on, Katy! Jump in!"

I shook my head, no. Josh stood several feet away from me. He was dripping wet. His wet clothes hung to his body. He hooped and hollered whenever someone jumped in. I wanted attention. I pulled myself up on the rock. Daddy yelled that I would get sick, but I didn't care. Josh's eyes were on me. That was all I had wanted.

I jumped.

The water enveloped me, burning at first then sinking in as icy chills. It pulled me down, tugging at my clothes and then sent me upward in a gush of water. I climbed to the bank. I looked up to see a hand reaching for me. Josh's hand. I gripped it. It meant nothing to him. He was just helping a girl out of the water. To me, it was contact. It was strength and warmth. Utter and complete captivation.

The day ended with hauling our sleeping bags into the old barn. We all fell into an exhausted sleep. And suddenly, the sun was peeking through the cracks in the wooden walls. We headed back to church the next day.

The week was full of activities. Silly youth activities. I just spent the majority of my time staying near Josh. I hoped that he didn't notice how much I liked him. I never really cared as long as I was near him. I filled my journal with ways and possibilities I could get near him. I "lived" him and breathed him all week. I tried to brush by his arm. I fell all over myself to sit near him. He was so wonderful. He was so full of life. Girls circled around him. He laughed and smiled at them. The pretty girls smiled in my direction. It was sympathy. I burned with more of a desire to make my presence known.

After a week of being rather dirty and messy, there was a dinner held on the second to last day. It was nothing extravagant, just a dinner where the guys escorted the ladies. It was meant to be an exercise for the young men to show chivalry. That was all it was meant to be, but I took it much further than that. I put on a yellow and green, silky, lacy blouse. I wasn't allowed to wear make-up yet, so I asked one of the other girls if I could borrow theirs. I powdered my freckled face. One of the girls squirted sweet smelling perfume on my clothes. I pulled my hair out of my face and curled the ends and whispered to myself, "You must look beautiful. So Josh will notice you." Yet, as I finished up getting ready, all I saw was a kid with braces and freckles trying to be someone she was not.

I knew that I would get the man I wanted. I knew I would get Josh. I'm sure he wasn't half as concerned about it as I was. I didn't know how the girls and guys would be paired together, but somehow I knew I would get Josh. I knew it.

The girls came down to meet the guys. My heart jumped into my throat when my eyes fell on the young man dressed in an orange shirt. His blond hair was spiked and his eyes twinkled. So handsome. The other guys couldn't compare to him in my eyes. My dad told all the girls to line up on one side and the guys on the other. I was surprised how easily I ended up right across from Josh. He had his hands clasped behind his back making his shoulders look even broader than they were.

"Ladies, the gentleman whom you are across from is your escort tonight," my dad said.

Perfection.

Yet, then I felt a pang of sadness. He would be disappointed that he had gotten me. He turned to me and I was surprised that he didn't look disappointed. If he was, he didn't show it. He walked toward me and offered his arm. I took it.

Heavens, I could hang onto this arm forever.

He smiled at me. His straight teeth gleamed.

Oh Lord, I love him.

In my naive mind, "love" was the only word that could describe my infatuation with him. I didn't see the difference between true, sacrificial love and what I was experiencing. Yet, there was most certainly a difference.

"You look nice," he said.

I almost choked on my own heart. Someone told us to smile and our picture was taken. That picture is one I would always wish I had. I had to let go of his arm to walk through the door to find our table. When I turned around, he was still standing at the door, his arm out.

"Excuse me, ma'am, but I'm supposed to escort you all the way," he said, smiling.

I gripped his arm and we walked to the table. I can still remember one thought as I hung onto his arm.

I want him to walk me down the aisle one day.

Then I chided myself for such a thought. He pulled my chair out as I sat. We ate and he picked all of his small tomatoes off of his salad.

It was over way too soon. Everyone was leaving and so I thanked Josh and he did some sort of silly bow. My silky shirt would smell like that perfume for weeks and I would bury my face in it from time to time, letting the memories of that night flood my mind.

The next day we loaded up and took off up the mountain to go canoeing. It was the last day of camp. We stopped along the New River. It's a beautiful river flowing through the countryside of the North Carolina Mountains.

The sun was warm on our shoulders as we grouped to rent canoes. Josh paid no attention to me. I tried to remind myself that I couldn't have him all the time. He walked up to one of the prettiest girls and I heard her immediately accept his offer of riding on his canoe. I felt sick. I chose another girl with whom I was a good friend and we took off. Josh was one of the first ones down the river. I was the last. My canoe scrapped the bottom of the river for miles. I tried to cheer up. But within a few minutes rain was pelting the inside of the metal frame. Lightning struck in the distance. We took on the bad weather as part of a great adventure and paddled harder. Once we arrived at our destination, we were dripping wet. The rest of the group waited under the trees. We were the last canoe to arrive.

We made it back to the church where the teenagers dispersed to go to their homes. Several of the kids needed a ride home, Josh being one of them. Several, as in six. So my Dad, sister and I, along with six others, packed into my Dad's old Ford Taurus. I walked into my bedroom at home and fell on my bed. The week was over and all that I had accomplished was becoming more dangerously enamored with Josh Isaacs.

The group of teenagers went to a senior living home a few weeks later. We set up a karaoke machine in the large living room of the home. The elderly people gathered around. It was quite a crowd. Josh and a few other guys, along with several girls sang. I squeezed in next to Josh. I had one thing to my advantage – I could sing. Even at my young age the others wanted me to lead. I felt pride rising in my chest. Yet, as I scanned the elderly people and their tired eyes, I felt guilty and disappointed in myself. I tried to dig down deep for some humility.

On the way back home we were piled in the van. I sat in front of Josh and he sat by another girl in the youth group. I knew she was "utterly in love" with him. I wanted to gag. He looked up at me and smiled. Then he did something very drastic … or so I thought. I felt heat run up my back as he slid his hand on her knee. She turned to him. Her face lit up.

He knew. For the first time, he made it very clear that he knew that I liked him. I didn't mean to, but I gave away my emotions with my eyes. Tears burned my throat. His face changed a little and he removed his hand from the girl's leg.

Josh had been living with a family from our church, so the van headed there to drop him off. When we got to the house, I got out of the car to take his seat. We were briefly in front of each other. In a moment of shear yearning and confusion, I pulled him into a hug. I don't know what I expected from him, but he didn't recoil. He hugged me back. I could feel his chin on my shoulder. We let go abruptly. I knew that everyone was staring at me, but no part of me cared. He turned to face me before he went in the door.

"I'll see you Sunday, okay?"

"Okay," I said.

I got back in the car and one of the girls said, "Oh, he is cute, isn't he?"

I just smiled and nodded.

I was obsessed with the blond 17-year-old. He was my last thought before I fell asleep and was often my first thought in the mornings. Though I knew better, I became even more consumed with him. I didn't even need his attention to strengthen my feelings. I "loved" him, and he was all I wanted. More than anything. Even more than God. My dad and mom may have known my feelings, though I kept them as secret as possible. Yet, if anyone had gotten hold of my journal, they would have known the truth. All of the truth. It was full of love letters to him. Neither of my parents said anything to me about it. They had no idea how many of my thoughts were of Josh.

Later that summer a mission team, including Josh and me, took off to Atlanta, Georgia. It started out as a rough trip. Dad had forgotten to load Kandace and my suitcases in the church trailer we were pulling behind one of the vans. Once we arrived in Atlanta, we realized that we would be heading to Walmart to get clothes. Disney clothes were on sale, so I ended up with several Mickey Mouse and Mini Mouse shirts. I was mortified. Josh smiled when he saw me and exclaimed, "I didn't know you liked Mickey Mouse!"

The mission team spent the week doing Vacation Bible School for a church there. Somehow I persuaded Josh to teach the music class with me. And somehow, he agreed. It was silly, really … Josh and me teaching little kids together. He mostly just kept everyone smiling. I loved being with him. I loved that he was willing to spend time with me.

The week ended and we were on our way home. Josh and I played "the hand slap game." I placed my hands on his flat, outstretched ones and he tried to gently slap the top of my hands before I could move them. Then I would take a turn. It never hurt. I loved it because my hands were on his. His strong hands. Finally, he forced me to stop because my hands were going to be bruised.

A pain gripped my heart though. I knew the truth. Josh didn't like me. Why would he? I was only 12-years-old. I was odd and awkward. He saw me as only a little girl. The worst part was that he was leaving, going off to seminary in the fall. Selfishly, I didn't want him to go anywhere, but I found peace knowing that he would come home often. It was only a couple hours away.

The summer was over. My mind was full of a fantasy world of Josh. I would often look down the gravel road that went past my grandparent's house and imagine us walking down it. The sun setting, the sky streaked in purple and pink and Josh holding my hand as we walked. It was a perfect vision to me. I imagined that over and over. It became my dream. I dreamed of being his. I wrote time after time in my journal that one day, one day he would say I love you. I practiced my name with his last name. Katy Isaacs. It sounded so perfect and yet so distant … so impossible.

I was giving my heart away. Somewhere inside of my soul, I knew it was dangerous. Yet, I gave it with full abandon to a young man who in no way loved me, nor ever planned to.

Infatuation

It was fall. Josh was gone. He was headed to Fruitland Baptist Bible Institute in Hendersonville, North Carolina. I wanted to cry and I did. I missed him before he had even left. I wanted to see him every Sunday and Wednesday like I used to. I wanted to see him at church, slinging little kids on his shoulders, making them laugh. I missed him so much. I wondered when I would see him again.

The first few months he came home often. I was satisfied. I knew little about what he was doing or where he was, but it didn't change the way I felt. I dreamed about the next time I would see him. I lay awake in bed at night imagining his face and praying for him. I was so proud of him. He was going to seminary after all. He would be a preacher. He would be the perfect husband. So, I continued to write in my journal. I wrote long letters to him.

One day I even ripped out one of the letters to him and slipped it in my Bible. I carried it to church and walked up to his Bible. It was lying alone on a chair and he was several feet away talking to someone. I pulled the note halfway out of my Bible. I fingered it as my mind battled, deciding what to do. I wanted to slip it in his Bible. I was ready. I knew what it said and I let the words I had written flitter through my mind.

"Josh, I just want to tell you how much you mean to me. I think about you all the time. I pray for you too. I just need you to know something. Josh, I love you."

I couldn't do it. I would look so foolish. He would never talk to me again. I left his Bible and when I returned home, I placed the note in the back of my journal.

Josh spent his days in seminary and working at a restaurant. He changed a little over time. He seemed less interested in talking to me when he was home. I smiled at him from across the aisle, when he was at church and he smiled back. Yet, somehow, things were different. I was slowly beginning to see that summer had taken with it many happy times with Josh … memories that would always stay just that … memories. Summer was gone, fall had … fallen. It had fallen hard.

Josh's presence became even more sporadic. He came around occasionally and the longer he was gone, the more my heart ached. I told myself that one day he would come back. One day he would love me as much as I did him. I prayed in my bed. I begged God for him. If I could have Josh, I would have all I needed.

Winter came and went. It was 2007. And summer came again. Vacation Bible School was in June, like always. Josh came and helped every day. He brought his precious little sister, Jasmine. The bubbly seven-year-old quickly became my friend. I truly loved the sweet girl. She reminded me of the way I looked at her age. She had the straight brown hair with thin bangs and round glasses. I spent a lot of time with her and Josh. I loved them both. Yet, Josh was still different. He was more distant.

After almost three years donning a metal mouth, I had my braces removed one day before VBS. My straight, white teeth drastically changed my appearance. And for the first time in a long time, I felt very pretty. Like usual, I cared if "one" person noticed … and he did. Josh smiled when he saw me. He immediately laughed when he noticed my new habit of constantly running my tongue over my glossy teeth. For the rest of that day I felt like things were how they had used to be. Josh laughed and it was wonderful.

The saying, "nothing good lasts forever" took on a strong meaning when I learned that Josh was in trouble. I didn't understand everything, but I heard Dad and Mom's voices downstairs in the living room. I pressed my ear against the door.

"He is immature," Dad said, "He just doesn't know how to handle money. He doesn't know how to manage his time. He isn't trying hard in school."

I didn't want to hear that. Dad didn't know the truth, but it was the truth. Josh hung on just enough to look like he was doing okay. He rarely came around anymore. Somehow I clung on to him. I still loved him.

September 4, 2007
You won't believe it. Dad was talking to Mom and he said that
the reason Josh hasn't been coming home on the weekends is because he
has been dating a girl. I wanted to throw up and die. Why? I couldn't
understand. Then Dad said that he had broken it off because he wasn't
ready for a wife. That raised my spirit, but still left a hole. Josh has not
dated any girl for a long time. Dad explained to Josh that he needs to
get through school before he begins looking. Josh turned 19 last month.
I wish I understood why I love Josh so much, because he doesn't love me.
Just being honest here. It hurts, but no matter what, I'll keep praying
for him. Dad said that he talked to him on the cell phone for a long
time yesterday. Dad, nor Mom knows how I feel, but I do and God
does. That is enough for me. Maybe one day Josh will see me for who
I am. Maybe. Oh dear God. Maybe!

I had been in the living room, straining to hear. I hadn't needed to see Daddy's face to know he was irritated. Mom listened
silently. I had clamped my hand over my mouth. For months and
years I had denied that Josh ever liked anyone, ever. I was persuaded
that he would love me. But here the truth smacked me across the
face, mocking me for every time I had claimed that I loved him.

A few days later my family and I went on vacation to the beach
on the North Carolina coast. I recorded in my journal these words:

September 9, 2007
Today is Sunday and we are at the beach and doing well. Yesterday
Josh called Dad's phone, but Dad wasn't close by, so I took it to Mom.
I didn't answer it. I saw his name on the Caller ID and I didn't know
which button to push to answer. He was one button away! Mom told
me to leave it on the table. Dad called him back and talked to him for
a long time. He came in and said that Josh was having some problems.
I prayed and prayed for him. My dreams were full of him. I hope he
is okay.

My family went to the beautiful Biltmore Estate in Ashville,
North Carolina and on the way home we visited Josh. It was September 20, 2007, a beautiful breezy Thursday. We pulled up to a
small barbeque restaurant in our minivan. There he was, getting

out of his car. He was so handsome. It had been a couple of months since I had seen him, and I just wanted it to be like old times.

It wasn't like old times. His face was unmistakable. He was not the free, funny Josh I knew so well. He seemed uncomfortable and anxious. He talked to Daddy a lot. I sat there. Mom, Kandace and Clara were talking. I wanted to talk to Josh, but he didn't want to talk to me. I ate my fries and sandwich in silence.

I denied the truth I had seen. I wrote in my journal later that night:

We visited Josh last night. He is doing well … he just has a lot to do. I didn't talk much. I knew if I talked I would lose control and just overflow with love! I am "just Katy" to him, but I still love him. I soaked in every moment so that I can't forget him if I don't see him for a while. I couldn't say "goodbye" because it sounded too final. I just smiled and waved. He hugged Mom and Dad, but I promise that I wanted to hug him the most. It just seemed too "forward" to hug him. I wish I would have said more to him. I miss him already!

The truth was that Josh wasn't there. Some gloomy version of him may have been there, but not the man I loved. He didn't say a single word to me. Whether I believed it at the time or not, he didn't even see me … I might as well have been invisible to him. I hopped up in the van and shut the door. I watched the car disappear around the corner as Mom buckled Clara in her car seat. Once we were headed down the road, Mom turned around to me and said, "You didn't say much, Katy."

I had not said a single word to him. Outwardly, I shrugged, yet inwardly I cringed. I wondered what had happened. Was something really wrong with him like Dad said? And that was when something changed inside of me. I was just a 13-year-old kid; of course I was nothing to him. I vowed to fill my journal with good things and hopes, but the truth sunk into my heart. Against all of my efforts, it seemed like my heart would break after all. I had to let him go before I ended up a broken mess.

Letting Him Go

By October, Josh was off the radar. He hadn't been to church in a long time and no one knew why. He was done. He was truly gone.

October 7, 2007

As I write I can't tell you how I feel. I have scratched for every bit of information on how Josh is doing because I don't ask Dad, as that will give him ideas. Josh was gaining so much respect. My love for him was becoming overwhelming and I prayed for him as much as possible. I feel sick. I have loved Josh for so long, but now I feel him slipping, slowly sliding away. Yet I never had him. Was all of this my imagination? Was I ever right to feel the way I did? He didn't even know about my love. Is this all you get out of love? A broken heart? He betrayed me without even knowing it! Why? Dear God, why? I loved him. I would have died for him. Why did I give my love to him? But at the time, he was everything. He was handsome, loveable, godly ... everything but mature. I was afraid that his immaturity would backfire on him, but he was doing fine! I believed he would make it when he became a sophomore in college. He failed us and he failed me. Will I ever see him again?? I don't understand! I love him. I love him. How can love come from a broken heart?

I stuffed that precious black notebook in my dresser drawer. Tears burned my eyes. My heart would take a long time to recover, but I knew that I had to begin to move on. At that point my emotion was sadness.

My emotion turned to anger. Several months later, when I hadn't seen or heard from Josh in nearly a year, I found my black journal. I flipped through the pages and laughed inwardly, yet, the depths of my heart still ached. The bitterness of the flesh took over and I scoured every inch of my room. I pulled out every piece of paper with his name on it, every little letter or note. Stuffing them in the journal, I tiptoed down the steps from my bedroom. I wanted a fire to burn them in. I wanted ceremony. I wanted to scream that I was done with that man. The paper shredder would have to do. It was by the washing machine. I closed the door behind me and began ripping out the journal's pages. I could only shred a few pages at once, so I watched a little bunch of pages after another slip through the shredder's teeth. There was one small piece of paper left. It was the note I had almost placed in Josh's Bible so many months ago. I read the last line of the neat handwriting.

Josh, I love you.

With a knot in my stomach, I ripped it to tiny pieces. I wouldn't let the shredder get to destroy that one. If I would have been alone in the house, I might have screamed and yelled, pretending that I was doing it all in his face. Instead I just let the tears fall silently as I tore the paper until not a single word could be read.

I walked away with an empty journal. I believed that as I had ruined those many words of love, that I had also destroyed any love I had in my heart for him. I didn't realize that there was still a small seed there inside of me. It promised that if it were ever to be watered, it would flourish. Yet, it also knew that it would never see water … not a drop. That "love" would wither, eventually.

My true love deserved to be saved for the man I would marry. My heart needed to be whole for him. Josh Isaacs would fade into the oblivion of my mind. After all, I had destroyed every trace of him in my life.

However, I had not destroyed every trace. A pink journal lay in an untouched drawer. It was the journal I had only rarely written in. It was also sprinkled with accounts of Josh. The black journal I had destroyed had been filled with letters to him, but the pink one had been full of my thoughts. I had forgotten about that little book. I wouldn't think about it again for years.

God mercifully allowed me to overcome that time in my life. If I could go back in time, I would have shared with my parents all that was stirring in my heart. I would have taken greater care to protect my heart. Josh never gave me a reason to believe that he liked me in return and I still chose to believe that he did care for me as more than a friend. Even though I was young, my feelings were real and strong, but because I was young, I couldn't handle them maturely. At 13-years-old, I wasn't ready to be married. In the end, my emotions were allowed to override my resolve. My heart could have been broken … but by God's grace, He protected me and taught me a lesson that I would never forget. From then on, I would wait on the one God had for me.

6
MY BROTHER

Another Sister

D addy always told us that he believed that he was supposed to have all daughters. So when my family immediately began the adoption process for another child from China, a little girl was what we assumed we would get.

The stack of paperwork began again in the last months of 2007 and into 2008. This time, however, Dad and Mom requested a "special needs" girl. The child could have had quite an array of needs. She could have had anything from minor heart problems to mental disabilities to missing limbs. With this vast assortment of special needs acceptable to my family, we were able to move through the adoption process at a brisk pace. It was determined that we would name the little girl, Carianne. I told everyone that I would call her Cari. I prayed for Cari every day. Like I had with Clara, I began to envision her with us. I imagined her.

It didn't take long for my parents to receive e-mails claiming that there were little girls available. The families they had originally been placed with had chosen other children, so those girls' pictures and information were sent to us. Each girl was given a temporary, American name.

On March 12, 2008 the agency sent out an email with several children's pictures. One of the little girl's names was Annie. She was almost five years old and had developmental delays. My parents requested more information, but another family who was further along in the adoption process quickly chose the little girl. There were other girls like Annie. Some had very serious health issues and others were chosen before we had a chance to learn more.

A Boy Instead

In May, the whole Chinese adoption "machine" began to churn very slowly. Most of the country's attention was on the Summer Olympics, which would take place in Beijing of that upcoming August. With the slowness of the process, my family explored other possibilities. Daddy finally determined that he would be willing to alter the paperwork to accept a girl or a boy.

My mind hadn't even ventured to imagine having a brother. Yet, it seemed that a boy was what God had in mind all along, because less than a week later, Daddy received a call. My journal entry showed my reaction.

May 21, 2008

A week ago today, Daddy got a call from the adoption agency saying that there is a boy available for us to consider. He has two clubbed feet. Which means that his feet are turned under. He is so cute! He is 16 days older than Clara and his name is Qing Bin Dang. Dad said that it would cost around $40,000 to get his feet repaired and we don't have that money. Mom got on the computer and found a hospital called Shriner's that said they could accept him as a patient and do the surgeries he would need for free. And the Shriner's Hospital closest to us specializes in repairing clubbed feet!

Sure, it all seemed good. It all appeared like there was no reason we should not accept this little boy. But this was Kevin Brown we were talking to. My father just never jumps into something unless he knows – unless he is sure it is God's will. We only had 48 hours until this boy would be shuffled through to another family. My daddy fasted and prayed. Yet, he told us that God hadn't shown him clearly. He wanted a clear answer. My daddy's faith was stronger than mine. I asked God to show Daddy something, yet deep down, I wondered if Dad would ever get his answer.

It was literally a few hours before we had to have an answer. Daddy was nowhere to be found. But God saw him. He was in his office in the basement, holding his Bible with his laptop before him. It was as though he expected God's answer just to pop up on the screen or to be highlighted in his Bible.

Dad prayed. He begged God to show him if Qing Bin was the one. Tears running down his face he murmured to heaven, "We are almost out of time." That is until the thought came to his mind: *The story account of the crippled man in the Bible!*

Qing Bin was "crippled" too and so maybe God would show him something in that story. Dad flipped his Bible open without even looking at it. His eyes were on his laptop as he searched online for where the story was in the Bible. He knew it was in one of the four Gospels, but he couldn't remember where. While he waited for the Internet to finally process and give an answer, he looked down at his Bible. His eyes didn't linger about the page. They hit these words:

Jesus Forgives and Heals a Paralyzed Man

He heard the Holy Spirit's voice. God was whispering to him. He told him to be like the four men in that story. Let our family be the four men who carried the crippled man to Jesus, so he could be healed and rescued. The crippled man had no chance of being healed without someone to bring him to Jesus. Qing Bin needed to be healed. He needed to be healed physically and spiritually. God's voice was clear. We were to bring him to Jesus.

I saw Daddy's face shining with joy when he walked up into the living room that day. He told us what had happened.

"I know for sure," he said. "We are supposed to go get Qing Bin. This little boy really needs us."

This little boy … he would be the one. After calling the adoption agency, we talked about names. Mom had always loved the name Andrew. She had always told us girls that if one of us had been a boy, we would have been named Andrew. For his middle name, everyone thought that the family name David should live on. My dad's first name was David, as was his father's. So it was decided that Qing Bin would be, Andrew David Brown. It seemed to be a rich, solid name. I liked it.

It surprisingly didn't take long for my parents to decide who would go to China. Since it was so expensive for our whole family to travel, Mama and Daddy decided that just two of us needed to go. Daddy decided to stay back and keep Kandace and Clara. Mom and I would go get my brother.

We were cooking chicken to sell at church to raise money for missions one day when Dad got a call from the adoption agency. He and I walked to the edge of the activity, so he could hear the woman over the phone. My heart dropped like a rock as I listened silently.

"So, are you saying that it is dangerous?" Daddy asked.

Once he was off the phone, I bombarded him with questions.

"The bottom line," Daddy said, "is that Andrew has a hernia. This hernia expands when he gets very upset and cries. It is possible that if he were to get very upset, it could rupture and become very toxic to his body. The lady was calling so that we would know and to inform us that he will need surgery as soon as possible once he is here."

"Is there anything not wrong with this child?" I let the words blurt out before I had a chance to process them myself.

"We need to pray that nothing happens until we can get it taken care of," Dad said firmly.

Getting Prepared for a Little Brother

In July, Kandace moved into my upstairs room. Some of my friends asked how we could stand it. But I just laughed and said, "It's not like we are going to poison each other!" Daddy built a wooden partition from some left over wood in the basement. It made us laugh to look at the differences from her side to mine. Her side of the room was hot pink and bright orange with glitzy pillows and beads everywhere. My side was lavender and a pale green. I had a few kerosene lamps and an old-fashioned vanity table. A floral quilt was draped over my bed to finish off that perfect country charm. We were very different to say the least. Yet, we got along very well together. We found that it was good for us to share. Mom and Dad often commented on how American children are far too accustomed to having their own everything, including rooms. Sharing a room made us more accountable and required us to think of someone else as we played music or left our lights on too late.

A couple of months passed as China built up for the Olympics. We were anticipating that we would get to travel to get Andrew in September. The adoption process generally required last minute travel planning and this trip was no exception.

August 26, 2008

Disappointment! The Chinese will not allow anyone adopting to travel during September because of the Olympics! The next dates to travel would be October 4th or 11th. I was so upset when I learned about this yesterday. My little brother is going to have to be in that orphanage for a little over 5 more weeks. I was angry with everyone involved. But this is the way it is and we have to keep moving forward. No turning back. Trusting in God.

August 28, 2008

Where do I begin? We got an e-mail saying that China may let us travel to China on September 13th after all! I was thrilled and I still am. Of course this is a big "maybe," but hey, at least we have a chance.

August 29, 2008

It's official! We're going to China on September 13th! I can't believe it! We better hurry up and get ready!

My family had scheduled our annual beach trip with my grandparents, Aunt, Uncle and cousins, for the week before the trip to China. On September 6th we left for Holden Beach. I had two suitcases. One was for the beach and the other was for China. The vacation was enjoyable, but in my heart, I was ready for China. On September 13th, we went straight from the beach house to the airport in Raleigh. Mama and I said goodbye to Daddy, Kandace and Clara and we took off to Washington, D.C for a short layover.

Finally, we arrived in Beijing. I could immediately see that this trip was going to be very different than the one with Clara had been. When we had arrived in China the first time to get my sister, we had seen many American families, but this time, it was just Mom and myself. We ended up in a junky, little van that went a million miles per hour down the road. I already felt tears. I knew that this was going to be a long ride and a long night. The hotel was nice enough. Yet I was exhausted and afraid, so I fell into a heap on those familiar "brick" beds and sobbed. Mom tried to comfort me, but I just wailed, "I want to go home."

The morning light made things feel better. And in a day, we were on another plane flying to Henan Province. Mom and I were the only two people from our travel group going to that province. It was odd how our guide, Fontana, seemed to moan a bit when she mentioned Henan. She said that it is the oldest province in China. Once we had landed, and rode through the city of Zhengzhou, I decided that it had to be the dirtiest province too. The city was eerie and dark. It wasn't the green and lush Hubei where Clara had lived. I felt even worse in Zhengzhou than I had in Beijing. We went to the hotel desk to exchange American money for Chinese money. They just shook their heads and said that they didn't do that there. Mom looked at Fontana and claimed that she was told the hotel would be able to exchange her money. Fontana hailed a taxi and we were off to the bank. The taxi's windows were rolled down, letting in the rankest smell. The smog and grime of the city became more apparent as we drove through it. The bank was the scariest place I had been to in China. Hundreds of people waited in line. We waited in line for hours. It was a rough start to the stay in Andrew's hometown.

The next day, we went to the supermarket and bought snacks for the hotel room. We ate at Pizza Hut and at a little restaurant called Prince Curry. While in China, getting Clara, the food had been very good. The worst thing I had eaten was duck and sushi. Prince Curry may have had an American name, but it wasn't anything like America. True to it's name, everything was full of the spice, curry. Mom wisely ordered an appetizer of potatoes and cheese. When the rude waiter laughed at her for ordering a safe "American dish" I gritted my teeth and pointed to something on the menu and said, "Well, I'll have this." I crossed my arms and smiled smugly. Mom just raised her eyebrows. The food came and Mama's was a nice circle of cheesy potatoes. Mine came and it looked like the restaurant's garbage from last week had been dumped on my plate. But I ate it. Forcing the spicy gravy down my esophagus, I asked Mom if I could have a bite of her food. Being the sweet mother she is, she relented.

I struggled to be happy in Henan Province. It was such a sad, dirty place. I watched the millions of inhabitants wander through the streets. I saw hundreds of hungry, homeless people on the side of the roads. Many had missing limbs or clubbed feet and I thought of Andrew.

He Never Cried

Only a few hours later, we packed up a few toys in a bag and joined Fontana to go get Andrew. I had no idea where we were going. We ended up on a street, ripped apart for construction. Smoke rose from below the ground and sewage ran down the gutters in the streets. We entered a gloomy building and met a man there who supposedly ran the orphanage Andrew was from. We walked up a narrow flight of stairs and turned down a long hallway. I could hear the pleasant sound of children. We were shown into a room with the first American families I had seen in Henan Province. Many were playing with their children for the first time. Little girls and boys smiling and laughing with their new parents. It made me happy to see hope and I prayed that Andrew would be happy as well. Nervousness surged through my veins as I scanned the room for my new sibling. My eyes landed on a tiny boy sitting on a little purple chair. He looked up and my eyes locked onto his. My brother. Mom immediately went down on her knees. He just chuckled to himself in a silly, innocent way. I hit the "record" button on the camcorder.

He was so adorable and he seemed pretty happy. My first thought was how different he looked in person. He was so skinny and yet muscular to be only 3½-years-old. We said "hello" to him.

He just looked at us with a slight smile. He propped himself up from a sitting position. Suddenly, he had propelled his little body upward and he was walking. His gnarled feet were flipped upside down and he easily walked around the room on the tops of his feet. Mom and I gasped. The nanny simply called him back. He didn't really listen, so she grabbed him up and placed him in front of us. I rubbed his skin and handed him a few of his new toys. He loved a small brown bear we had brought and cuddled and played with it.

Andrew was so dirty. I was nearly convinced that he had never had a bath. He had sores on his skin. On his forehead there was a dark blue bruise. Mom signed a few papers at a desk in the back of the room. I played with Andrew and laughed as he pulled a wad of hard candy out of his shirt pocket. We assumed they were a gift from his nanny. He popped a jawbreaker in his mouth periodically.

I loved this little boy. As I picked him up and held him against my chest, he just played with his new bear and my heart melted.

Mom took care of a lot of things that I didn't understand, nor had to be involved in. Eventually, the nanny swung him up onto her hip. Fontana said that it was time to leave. I was ready to leave that building. We walked down the hall to a small elevator that looked like it didn't have the strength to lower us a single floor. Once inside, I began to hear soft weeping. I looked back at the nanny holding my brother. Tears rolled down her thin cheeks as she cradled him and pressed her head to his. I hadn't given much thought to how she must have felt until that moment. She had given so much for Qing Bin and she was sad to let him go. She began to speak to Fontana and Fontana turned to us to translate.

"She said that if Qing Bin cries very hard, his hernia may rupture."

Goodness. I just stared while Mama nodded.

The nanny talked on. Fontana translated. "She said that he always cries when I leave him and so he will cry this time too. You need to calm him down. Give him whatever he wants so that he doesn't cry."

Mom and I looked at each other. Worry must have flooded both of our faces. We walked out of the building and down the spooky street toward the taxi. My panicked mind began to imagine all of the terrible things that could happen if Andrew broke into a tantrum. I tried to remain calm. I was sure a tantrum was coming.

The nanny handed Andrew off to Mom as we slid into the back seat of the taxi. She cringed as though she expected him to begin to cry. But he didn't cry. He just sat there quietly between Mama and me with his bear. He didn't smile or cry. The taxi sped away and I waited for Andrew to turn around, look for his nanny and scream. He didn't. All the way to the hotel he just sat there. My little brother sat there without a care in the world. And it hit me that this little boy had nothing. He owned nothing. He was handed to us with the clothes on his back and candy in his pockets. He had no one but us. I suddenly felt a distinct longing to protect and love this little boy in every way possible.

We pulled him out of the taxi and carried him up to our room. He didn't cry. He just looked around at his surroundings. I suppose that after getting Clara and dealing with her days of screaming and crying, I was expecting the worst. Yet, Andrew was different and he just laid down on one of the beds. After a few minutes of playing with his new toys, he fell asleep and slept for 14 hours.

We were amazed at his calm disposition. The next morning he woke up, forcing his little eyelids open in a way I would come to always love about him. I, yet again, braced myself for a tantrum. But he didn't throw one. He just played with his toys and drank a little box of milk. The water turned brown as we gave him a bath. He loved the water and splashed and played.

At the hotel's breakfast buffet Andrew ate and ate. I ate too, until I saw a grasshopper on our table. I assumed it had come in on the flowers in the vase, but I was still rather disgusted. Andrew happily picked his way through the packs of assorted jellies and opened one after another. He licked the sweet jelly out until there wasn't a nary bit left. He smiled gleefully.

We spent most of our time sightseeing and enjoying eating Pizza Hut every day. There were rare occasions where we went to McDonalds or Starbucks … but Pizza Hut was our favorite. The petite Chinese ladies would smile when we entered the restaurant and say, "One American Special and two Pepsies?" We would nod, trying to hide our embarrassment.

My new brother learned the ropes. We pulled out pictures of Clara, Kandace and Daddy and told him who each person was. He laughed and smiled as he stared into the shiney picture of Clara.

Andrew proved that he wasn't always content and showed a whiny side. He would blink his eyes tightly to produce tears. But even his worst pity parties were cake walks compared to what we had experienced in China with Clara. I was thankful–more than thankful, for the way Andrew found trust in us.

We were overjoyed to board the plane home. Andrew curled up in the seat between Mama and me and fell asleep for 11 hours. He slept all night and when the plane landed in the wee morning hours, he sat up and looked around with delight. America smelled sweet as we dragged our cramped and aching muscles through the airport. Daddy was off in the distance. His bald head gleamed in the bright lights. He looked down at Andrew and with all the love an earthly father can possess, he said, "Welcome home, Son." To hear Daddy say "Son" made me want to cry. It reminded me of heaven, somehow.

My brother had spent 3 1/2 years crawling on his gnarled hands and knees across the filthy orphanage floors. He had been left alone and hungry. Dirty, abandoned and in no hope of physical healing, my brother had struggled through life. The signs were evident in his small stature, lack of speech and immature movements. But Andrew David Brown looked at life with a glisten in his weathered eyes. He had been through the misery, so the blessings were even more beautiful to him that they had ever seemed to me.

In the first few weeks home, he fell in love with our family. He had the first of several surgeries on his legs and had his hernia repaired. He never complained. Andrew became the brother that God always intended we would have. His story is one that even the toughest hearts feel pricked by. He was indeed rescued by my family, but more importantly by his Father who loved him when we were huddled alone and afraid in the depths of that dirty city.

Clara and Andrew. They are my China babies. Without them, life would never have been whole. They taught me that adoption is one of life's greatest miracles. Taking care of orphans is one thing that Jesus called "pure religion." He thinks it is beautiful. He thought it was so beautiful that He made a way for me to be adopted too ... into His family as a child of God. Those years of adoption revealed to me the mercies of God. Watching my mama and daddy's unbending, unchanging pursuit of love and trust in my siblings guided me to the feet of my Father who pursues my heart with even more love than that. "Family" isn't just the blood that runs through the veins. It is the love that binds the hearts. Family is forever.

A Different World

Some people seem never to come to the realization that the world is for more than just meeting their needs. Some never see past themselves. I never wanted to be one of those people. As a child I always wanted to reach others ... to be an example. Too bad I was a far cry from what I should have been. I wasn't a bad person, but I certainly didn't see how much need there was. Even after adopting two siblings from China, I hadn't truly grasped the acts of mercy, of grace, and of selfless love.

Besides that, I had never been truly alone. I never had to choose to give others all I could give without looking back. I never had to look into the face of Almighty God and say, "Okay, it's just You and me." Shortly after my 15th birthday I would, and my view on life would permanently change.

The continent of Africa was calling my name. In the months leading up to May 2009, my dad and I prepared for a trip to Ethiopia. My father had learned of mission work going on there from a professor at Southeastern Baptist Theological Seminary in Wake Forest, North Carolina. Dr. David Black is an author of several books on the New Testament and Greek. My dad learned about him from a mutual friend. Dr. Black and his wife, Becky Lynn were missionaries to Ethiopia. Becky Lynn spent the first 12 years of her life there as part of a missionary family. Dr. Black came to speak at my church on the book he had written, *The Myth of Adolescence*. He mentioned their work in Ethiopia. My dad was captivated after learning about it. I, too, was taken.

A few months later, we were packing for the trip. I wasn't stuffing bathing suits and cute clothing in my bags. Rather, there were mosquito nets, rat repellent powder, peanut butter and many long, plain skirts. I cringed at the thought of not having a shower for days on end. The thought of nastiness bothered me greatly. Yet, I prepared lessons for the children and youth. They were long, well-planned lessons. My excitement grew. I knew very little of what to expect from this far-away country, but I was ready for anything … or so I thought.

On the bright morning of May 23, 2009, I lugged my suitcase down the stairs of my comfy home. I tearfully kissed my family goodbye and rode away beside Daddy. We picked up our two other team members: a lady from our church named Amber and a dear friend of my dad's, who would quickly become my friend as well, Dale Jennings.

After two hours and a stop at Krispy Kreme Donuts, we were at the Raleigh Airport. We saw Mrs. Black and the other three team members from her church. We were shuffled through security and before long we were boarding the plane. It landed a little over an hour later in Washington, D.C. And finally, it was time to board the plane leaving the U.S. I looked back as I stepped on the plane, taking a deep breath of the sweet air. We flew for ten hours. I was quickly beginning to feel a sense of anxiousness. The little screen on the back of the seat in front of me had a map on it. It constantly reminded that we were moving hundreds of miles away from home. The little plane on the map inched towards Rome, Italy where we landed for a short layover. In seven more long hours, the pilot announced our landing in Addis Ababa, Ethiopia's capital city.

It really hadn't begun to sink in until we stepped off of the plane into the smoky, smelling airport in the center of Ethiopia, that the dim, gloomy airport was a far cry from anything American.

But I would later find that it was the most "American" building I would see for a long time.

I didn't want to take a step outside. Unfamiliar faces surrounded me. Someone pulled my backpack off my shoulder. I panicked as I watched my bag disappear. I was hugged and kissed from all directions.

My head was spinning. A bus loomed ahead. Was that the bus we would take? I had the feeling that I would never see light again as I stepped on the bus with dining room chairs for seats.

Everyone around me talked and laughed. I wanted to scream. Daddy seemed so relaxed. Everyone seemed … happy. It was so dark outside that I couldn't make out much of Addis Ababa. The bus stopped in front of a tall metal gate. A man opened it. Behind the tall wall sat a house. The guesthouse. The beautiful cottage I had imagined was not there. Instead, it was a crooked house surrounded by a wall with sharp-coiled wire and shards of broken glass at the top. We piled out of the bus. My missing backpack landed at my feet along with my suitcase. I stepped aside as everyone buzzed around me. I was mortified, terrified and unable to move. No one noticed the tears streaking my face in the darkness and they were too busy to notice when we stepped into the house. One thought kept resounding in my head: *This is only the beginning.*

My bags were placed in a room with a bunk bed and a king size bed. Being the youngest of the three women on the trip, my bag was tossed onto the top bunk. I was content with that. It was far from everyone – where I could think and cry.

I wanted Daddy. I needed someone familiar, someone to comfort me. I pulled him aside and dragged him into the ladies bedroom while everyone was in the living room. I couldn't talk. I just let his steady arms hold me as I sobbed. He told me that it would be okay. He told me something he had said a million times before when I had been afraid in my bed as a little girl:

"Things will look better when the sun comes up."

I gathered fresh clothes and headed to the bathroom. Mrs. Black's voice was behind me.

"Oh Katy, there is no hot water now."

So, I selfishly stood there till someone proclaimed there was warm water. I would be the first to be clean. I would feel better even if everyone else stayed filthy.

I laid awake on my bunk until the sun peaked over the horizon. Though exhaustion pulled me to sleep, fear held me awake. I sobbed into the pillow until tears wouldn't come. I squeezed my eyes closed and prayed that when I opened them I would be in my room in North Carolina. This place even made China feel American. I knew there were little villages scattered around the town of Alaba, 126 miles from the guesthouse where I was. Those villages would be filled with children – children that I needed to teach. It was so overwhelming to me. I didn't want to fail. I prayed the staple prayer of my life.

God, help me not be afraid.

He did. In the rickety bed in Addis Ababa, God was there and He surrounded me. He promised He wouldn't leave me. I believed Him. Sleep came as the sun gleamed through the curtains. Daddy had been right. Things did look better when the sun came up.

Less than an hour later, the familiar aroma of French bread and maple syrup greeted me along with the scent of mangos and fried bananas. I happily ate with the other shining faces from our group around the table in the guesthouse. The house proved to be a lovely place after all, mismatched and surrounded by flowers and birds.

The day was full of visiting historic buildings in Addis. I was wondering what we would have for lunch and about that time we were led into probably one of the nicest restaurants in Ethiopia. The smiling Ethiopian man across from me, whom the Blacks called Nigusse, ordered our food in a speedy, smooth voice. From where I was sitting, it looked like a pizza was on the waiter's arm as he walked to the table. It was indeed a metal pizza pan, but when he lowered it, I realized how wrong I had been to assume. The pan was covered in flat, gray, bubbly bread. Piles of different sorts of meat were evenly placed along the bread. I was given a napkin, which I placed in my lap. It was wet. I looked down to see that it was a rolled up version of the gray bread. Nigusse pulled the bread apart and sopped up the meat and popped it in his mouth.

Easy enough.

I pulled a piece of the soggy bread off and dipped it in the meat. The smell was okay. I silently took pride in the fact that I was not a "picky eater." It was never because I naturally loved to eat different foods, but rather, because my mom and dad had never allowed anything else. They said that whatever was placed before me, I would eat. I would eat it thankfully. So I had grown up never understanding how other children were allowed to eat only pizza, chicken nuggets and fries just because they were deemed "picky." I had decided that American children really aren't picky; they are allowed to be picky.

So, I plopped the meaty bread in my mouth. All of my pride vanished in a single instant. The gray bread was gritty and extremely sour. The meat was "different," but easy to swallow. The bread hung in my throat as through my stomach wanted no part of it. Someone asked if I liked the injera. Injera. Mrs. Black's words from our training came back to me like a dictionary definition. Injera: Bread made of a grain called teff, mixed with water and set to ferment for days. The definition didn't do it justice.

"Oh yes, it is delicious!" I said cheerfully. Not.

Alaba Kulito

Joyful was not the word to describe me as I crawled over the side of the bed the next morning. I huffed that the sun wouldn't be up for another three and a half hours. I handed my suitcase to Daddy as I stepped onto the bus. We would begin our six-hour drive to Alaba Kulito. As the sun peeked over the horizon and we said farewell to the mountains of Addis, I noticed we stepped further and further back into another time period as we drove. Women in colorful skirts and shirts carried packs of grain and baskets of every imaginable Ethiopian food on their heads.

Finally, Mrs. Black called out happily, "Welcome to Alaba!"

I turned to look out the window, my eyes blurry from sleep. The dirt road was lined with shanty stores. Cardboard, metal, and bits of plastic made up what surrounded me. Horses and buggies mingled with little blue vehicles that buzzed in and out of side roads like ants on an anthill. People were everywhere. Children were everywhere. The bus turned down a side road and stopped in front of a green gate. A smiling woman was behind it. The cute, little house behind must have belonged to her. The brick and stone house was large compared to what I had seen in the area.

She opened her arms to us as we stepped down from the bus. *"Tenestaline!"*

The lady standing before me, dressed in beautiful, colorful, mismatched clothes, was Marta. She welcomed us into her home. The floor was slick with kerosene, which I later learned is their floor cleaner. Overstuffed chairs were a pleasant sight. Our luggage was unloaded and we were shown our accommodations. I had been wondering where we would stay. Only Dr. Black, Dale Jennings, Dad and I would stay in Alaba, while the rest of the team rode another 13 hours to Burji in the deep, southern mountains of Ethiopia, mere miles from Kenya.

In the compound where the house was, there were small rooms all in a maze. The rooms were what many would consider guest rooms or even servant quarters. I started to follow Dr. Black and Mr. Dale around the back of the main house. I expected we would all be in close proximity. Nigusse stopped me. My dad and I would be staying in the neighboring compound. Well enough.

We followed Nigusse out to the dirt street and to the next gate. Another house much like Marta's and her husband Demessie's was there. Young girls scrubbed clothes in a metal bowl filled with brown water on the doorsteps. The sound of cattle and sheep met my ears and we followed the sounds. One of the rooms behind the house was filled with animals. The stench was stifling. Flies attacked my face as Nigusse opened the door in front of me. I ducked under the four-foot tall opening. The room I was in was completely dark. Daddy pulled me toward him. Something in the corner rattled as I heard a mouse … or a rat screech away. Nigusse flipped the light switch. A single light bulb on the ceiling provided a dim glow. The room contained a lumpy bed and a small table. The room's floor slanted downward. Daddy and I were left there just in time for the power to go out. We learned that the government controlled the electricity and it could be turned off at any time. I pulled the sheet back from the single window only to allow a swarm of flies into the room. Daddy found a flashlight in his bag.

We found the restroom. It wasn't a restroom to me. It was connected to the sheep pen. It was a hole in the ground. Just dirt and mud that slipped down into a deep hole. It was covered with every imaginable bug in the world, or almost every imaginable bug. A sheet was hung on the grassy-reed wall as a door. The smell made me gag every time I walked by it, much less entered it. I quickly learned to distinguish when I needed to go to the restroom and when I really needed to go. Because one should never go unless they absolutely must! The shintabet (the word for restrooms in Ethiopia) is a word I would not easily forget.

I didn't take time to unpack. I wanted to see everyone. I wanted to see Alaba and Alaba wanted to see me. The church was right across the road, so each night many of the elders and members came to eat with us in Demessie and Marta's house. The table along the wall was laden with noodles and meats and injera. There was a bowl of red chili peppers called "berbere." The thick sauce was poured all over my noodles like spaghetti. The heat of the peppers was like an electrical shock in my mouth, yet I actually liked it.

I watched Marta. She was never still. Always working. Her son, Tekalen, came to me holding a bowl and a pitcher. He bent over and poured sweet-smelling water over my hands. He did the same to everyone else. The girls of the house were plentiful. I couldn't begin to figure out who was a daughter, a cousin or friend, but they all served as well. They sat us down in the nice furniture and they sat in the corners and wherever there was room. We asked them to sit with us, but they refused, claiming there would not be enough room. These people were truly servants. They were not servants because we were white Americans, but because we were their guests, their brothers, and I … their sister.

I began to see that these people were different from any people I had ever known. They gave everything and expected nothing in return. They were hospitable with their arms open wide. They had a quality I had always considered I possessed myself. Sacrificial. Yet, I was beginning to see that I was nothing of the sort.

Thus was the first day. And actually, it was good. If I wanted to consider what I had already experienced amazing, then what I would encounter in the next eight days would be beyond incredible.

Softening My Heart

Cows.
The sound of cows wanting something desperately.
Probably food.
I want food too.

I opened my eyes to see darkness, almost as dark as the backside of my eyelids. Monday morning I awoke beside Daddy. It was so good to be with Daddy, but I soon realized that day I would be alone.

Alone.

Not really alone. Dr. Black would be teaching the adults inside the church in the village where I would be teaching the children, but I wouldn't have Dad there beside me. He would be going to teach in the church across the road. I would be getting in an old, rattly Toyota Land Cruiser and be taken to a village, which name I couldn't even pronounce.

An hour later, I was sitting in Marta's living room. Daddy had left to go teach in the church. I sat with my black bag on my lap. My Bible, notes, bottled water and tissues were all neatly stashed.

"Oookay! Keety! It iss time to go!" Nigusse bellowed.

So I left. The ride was long and suddenly all the plastic and metal and cardboard were gone. What now made up the homes I passed were the most natural materials known to man ... dirt, hay, sticks, and any other thing that could be pulled off of the ground. These were huts. Every Westernized thing I could think of was absent here. I had stepped back into a time period I had only read about; but suddenly, all I wanted was to become a part of this place, for a while at least.

The Land Cruiser pulled up in front of a mass of people. I gulped. There were so many and they banged on the sides of the vehicle. Would they attack me? I didn't want to get out. Could I teach through the window?

But Dr. Black hopped down and greeted the masses. David, who was the "mother church's" pastor and my translator, helped me crawl out and jump down onto the dusty soil. The smiles were everywhere. Bright teeth behind dirty faces.

Dirty.

That word hardly did justice to describe what I saw. I would be lying to say that I kissed each child and pulled them into my arms in that first village. My heart still held a somewhat hard, unapproachable exterior.

If these people can't be clean and smell nice, then why should I get near them? If I am ever bound to get lice, it will be here. Ugh. I hate lice.

Satan's evil forces whispered little lies in my head. Things just small enough to curb my strength. Things just big enough to keep me from doing my best. I smiled. A beautiful little girl came up to me. Her eyes sparkled. But when I saw her mouth, I felt Marta's noodles from breakfast gurgle in my stomach. The little girl's mouth was covered in open, infected sores. Dozens of flies swarmed her face. She grasped my hand and smiled. And my heart melted a little.

The children were finally settled and gathered and sitting on wooden benches outside of the village church. There were at least 30 children and they piled on top of one another. They stared at me. At me.

"It is time to start, Keety," David said from beside of me.

I slipped the black bag off of my shoulder and laid it at the base of the tree behind me. And I began. I taught stories from the Bible. I sang with them. I tried to remember to make everything exciting.

After a while, the kids started to get restless. David gently whispered that perhaps we should play a game. I felt heat rise up my back. Was I ruining everything? Was I making the Bible seem boring? What game should we play?

Duck, Duck, Goose. It was the first game that came to my mind and the open field, where we stood, was a perfect place to play. The little smiling faces quickly learned how to play the fast-paced game. They touched each head as they walked around the circle of children saying, "Dook, Dook, Dook, Goose!!"

I loved it. Their dirty hands touched my head and the little girls pressed against my clothes, but it was okay. I didn't mind. And then I taught again. The nervousness came and went, but a new emotion hit me when I turned to pick up my black bag to remove a lesson picture. The bag was literally moving. Ants. So many huge, red ants.

"*Remain calm,*" I screamed in my mind.

I held it together long enough to finish teaching and then I kicked my bag, letting the ants fly off in a thousand different directions.

Dr. Black came out of the church along with the other adults of the village. He seemed so joyful. He knew how to do all of this. He came to me and the kids stared in an awe-reverence.

"How did it go?" he asked.

"Good." I smiled.

He turned toward the kids and began singing. It was an Ethiopian song. His deep voice resounded along the quiet meadow. The faces of the children radiated pleasure. They sang too and I hummed and clapped, as I felt tears burn my eyes. The sound was heaven or the closest thing I had ever heard to heaven.

The ladies of the village came to me. They shook my hands and kissed my cheeks. Most of them were so small. My average height of five feet, five inches seemed to dwarf everyone. Though they were small and thin, their hearts were huge. They showed me that they were so thankful, so happy that I was there.

I felt God begin to whisper into my mind, "Ah, child. Do you finally see how much bigger the world is? Do you finally see that serving – that giving – is better than receiving? Watch and learn from these people. They have more than you can possibly know. These people have Me."

That night I sat on the couch in Demessie and Marta's house. Their daughter Rannie bounced around me in a giddy happiness. Her voice lifting lilting Amharic music to my ears. I was quickly learning that I loved their music. It was a hearty, rich sound.

I pondered how we Americans can sit on our pews in elegant churches and the sound that we lift to heaven is little more than half-hearted. I pondered how we could clasp our clean hands in front of our clean clothes and sing with stone faces with all that God has given us.

These people may be dirty. Yes, they may be thin. They may be tired. But they sing. They raise their hands. They weren't ashamed to make a joyful noise.

So, I decided as I sat in the massive church service one of the Sundays we were there, I had to change. As I watched over 2,000 men and women and children piled onto the hard benches of the church with their voices raised in praise, I chose to be like them. I decided that when I returned home, I wouldn't let the tradition of the American Church ruin my worship to God. I would sing, I would raise my hands in worship and I would not be ashamed.

The Breaking Point

When you have a plan in your head as to how things are supposed to happen, any little thing that deviates from that plan is uncomfortable. I am the kind of girl who always has a plan. I want to know what will happen, but I prefer to design what will happen. Well, God doesn't really work that way. He chooses what happens and the first Thursday of our trip was no exception.

Honestly, I rely on my journal for a lot of what happened that day and the few that followed. It has become a blur in my memory, yet that blur has burned a memory in my mind that I will never forget, nor do I want to.

On that warm day, the cows, sheep and goats bleated like they had all the mornings before, but the animals hadn't awakened me. The alarm had. Daddy's alarm clock beeped. I waited for Dad to turn it off, but he didn't. I leaned over him to feel into the darkness for the clock and turn it off. As I pulled back, I could feel that Daddy was sweaty. Heat radiated through his t-shirt.

"Daddy?"

"Yes?" His voice was weak.

"Are you okay?"

"I am not sure. I just don't feel very good," he answered, sitting up.

Oh no. Sickness. My mind already started to race.

He pulled himself over the side of the bed and stood up. "I'll be fine."

I prayed so. Daddy had hundreds of people counting on him to teach. He seemed sluggish all morning. It appeared to take all of his power to eat the food Marta had prepared. The pale shade of his normally pink cheeks was a telltale sign. Daddy walked to the church and I was left to wait for the Land Cruiser to pick me up.

Once I arrived back at our room for lunch, I found Daddy on the bed. He was so still it spooked me. He woke up when he heard me. He still felt very bad.

Yay, I thought. *Just what we need … sickness.*

I had no idea how very down hill things would go. Dad rested until he had to go back and teach. It was all he could do to walk straight.

One glimpse of my father after the long afternoon apart gave me a clear answer: Dad was worse. Was it the water? Was it the food? What on earth was wrong? Daddy tried to fellowship with everyone, but with each passing moment, he slipped further. After a while, we went to bed. He fell into a fitful sleep. I stayed as far on my side of the bed as I could. I heard the door creak open and Dad step outside. The flashlight flickered down the dirt trail to the restroom. I cringed as I imagined him in the rank stall as sick as he was. He came back. I knew he was sick. He fell into the bed. I prayed that a few hours would make him better.

That morning I awakened to the sound of an obnoxious cow. I rolled over. I suddenly realized that the alarm clock hadn't gone off. I hadn't set it. The clock blinked that I had awakened just in time to have enough time to get ready. I quietly thanked God for the annoying cow.

Daddy still hadn't moved. He looked like he was made of wax. Pasty and eerily quiet.

My long, lost enemy, Fear, emerged from the abyss.

He is dying.

I shook the thought. Yet, I was shaken. I had never seen Daddy like that. What was I supposed to do? It was almost time for breakfast and he obviously couldn't teach. But all of those people were counting on him ….

I quickly got ready and grabbed my black bag. I whispered to Daddy that I would be gone for just a few minutes. He nodded. I walked down the street and into Demessie and Marta's courtyard. I had never been through the long maze behind their house, but in my mind I replayed Mr. Dale describing where their rooms were. I knocked on the door, hoping it was the right one. Dr. Black opened the door.

"Katy! Are you okay?" he asked.

I felt like a tiny child. "Daddy is sick. Really sick. I don't know what to do."

He grimaced. Mr. Dale heard from his adjoining room and joined us. Dr. Black rummaged through a First Aid box. He picked a few items and followed me to our room. Daddy looked up when we entered and sat up slowly.

Dr. Black asked him how he was doing. I just stood there. I held back every tear and sob that was aching to explode from my insides. Daddy mumbled something. Dr. Black gave him some medicine and told him to rest. It was like a tidal wave in my chest. Tears and fear swelled.

"We are going to leave now," Dr. Black said.

I let my eyes fall back on Daddy. He was slouched. He almost looked withered. I had to leave him. I had to go. I threw my arms around him. Then the sobs came. Gripping his damp shirt, I clung to him.

"It will all be alright, Kate. Be strong," he whispered in my ear.

Choking back sobs, I straightened my clothes and wiped my face with a tissue. I joined Dr. Black and Mr. Dale, since they had stepped outside while I cried.

"Are you okay?" Dr. Black asked.

"I am." And somehow, I was. God gave me a smile for my face. I reminded myself that the children in the villages I would visit needed to see Jesus in me, no matter my circumstances. I taught the lessons in front of the crowds of children and young people. I moved my arms, I sang, I jumped and played. The strong sun kissed our faces and God must have smiled, as I loved the children.

My translator at that village was a teenager named Muhammad. He had been a murderer who had recently become a Christian. At the time, I felt unsure of having him as my translator, yet I quickly realized how wrong I had been. He was the sweetest, most humble young man. Truly a new person.

I was amazed at the differences that stretched across the villages where I taught. Many had their very own language. One or two had rarely, if ever, seen a white person. Each village was especially unique in its own way.

At lunchtime, when we returned to Alaba, I was anxious to know how Daddy was doing. The day had reached an uncomfortable temperature. I silently wished for a nice long shower. When I stepped into our room, the heat hit me like a wave. It was at least 90 degrees in the dark room. The tin roof was absorbing the sun's heat and causing the small room to heat up like an oven. My eyes eventually adjusted to the darkness. The room smelled of sickness. On the table by the bed sat two glass Sprite bottles and a bowl of soup. I asked Daddy how he was doing as I laid a damp cloth on his head. He weakly replied, "Not too good."

I nodded and turned away, trying to act calm. I had had enough. I felt a feeling I had never felt before. True loneliness. One could argue that I wasn't really alone. There were other team members just a house away. I wasn't really by myself, but nevertheless, it is impossible to explain how I felt it was the darkest loneliness I had ever experienced. For just a few moments I leaned against the wall and let the fear take over. I was too weak to fight it, or so I thought.

Daddy is dying.

I kept trying to shake the thought, but it held fast. I pressed my palms to my eyes. Tears burned in my throat like fire.

I am going to be here all alone. Daddy is going to die and I will be stuck here. He will never live through this.

My incoherent mind ran wild. Parasites. Daddy must have parasites. Or he could have picked up a remote African disease that his body can't fight off. I remembered that my father had been born very premature. He had always struggled to get well from any sickness because of his weak immune system.

What if this is too much for him?

I literally felt my knees going weak. I looked at the clock. I had about an hour before I had to go to the next village. I wanted to lie down … but where? The suitcases were stacked in the corner of the room. I pulled them out and laid them side-by-side. The torture of fear surrendered long enough to give me some rest. I fell asleep.

Colorful Skirts

I jolted awake at the creaking of the door. I sat up quickly. I completely expected to see Daddy's tall silhouette against the bright sunlight. Instead, a small woman entered. Two other women followed. My first thought was that they had accidentally entered the wrong room. Yet, when they looked at Daddy, they seemed confident that they were in the right place.

I hopped up.

"Daddy? We have some company." I gently prodded Daddy awake.

Daddy sat up, as though it took every ounce of his strength. He didn't say a word.

I said hello to the ladies. They didn't even seem to notice me. They were looking at the ceiling. As the sun shown through the door they hadn't shut, I recognized their faces. These were some of the ladies from my Daddy's class he had been teaching.

One of the women's voices broke through the silence. It was a rich, melodious sound. It was a sound that I will never forget. Her face was wet with tears and turned to heaven. She grabbed at her skirt. That was when I noticed their skirts. Color began to swirl. The long colorful skirts spun as the first lady prayed. She was praying for Daddy. It was as though she were looking into the very face of God. She moved and swayed as she prayed. Her hands raised; she cried out in Amharic. The other two women did the same. They spread out across the small room. I stood out of their way as they swirled, prayed and cried.

This was faith. This was prayer. This was the absence of fear. I let the tears roll down my face. I didn't bow my head. I raised it to heaven as they did. Daddy sat on the bed. The sickness was so strong that he didn't even acknowledge what was happening. They may have been praying for him, but I was the one who experienced the presence of God. I was the one who felt the peace. I wondered for a moment if it was a dream. But it wasn't. It was too good to be just a dream.

The women slowly quieted down and let their skirts fall limp. They each looked once more at my daddy and said something to heaven. And as quickly as they had come … they were gone.

My whole mindset changed. Those ladies had been the hands of God, reaching in to give me hope and peace. A song came to my mind. It was a new song, one that God had given to me. I scribbled down the words and promised Jesus to write that song one day.

You're Enough for Me
When tears are my offering
Or When Joy is My Song

Daddy began to recover almost immediately. It took him several days to get strong, yet he was able to continue teaching the next day. He later remembered that though we were provided with bottled water, he had accidently taken some of the tap water, which was unsanitary for our American stomachs. God brought him through. God brought me through.

One of the last days in Alaba, Dr. Black and I went to a village on a mountain. It was the village I will always remember most, especially considering it was quite a climb. The rugged Land Cruiser drove as long as it could climb up the narrowing trail. Finally, we got out to walk the remainder of the way. We jumped over rocks and avoided cliffs. Once we arrived, I was breathless. The beautiful sight of Alaba below was worth the climb.

I met a blind girl there, whose family had died. Only her brother remained and he spent much of his time farming and working to provide for them. The sweet, 15-year-old girl was so thin and solemn it broke my heart. I gave her a hug and had a translator tell her that I loved her dearly and I would see her again. I meant it.

A few days later, we went to the last village. That last village was harder to leave than any of the others. It was, after all, the last. The Ethiopian dirt puffed up as the tires rolled over the bumpy trails. I waved out the window. The cool air licked my face as the children ran by the side of the Land Cruiser to grasp my hand. I called out, "I LOVE YOU!" And their many voices echoed mine. They had stolen a piece of my heart and I wanted them to have it always.

The next morning, I kissed the faces of my new friends. I put away my lessons for the last time. I packed my suitcase. I said goodbye and promised to come again.

I marveled at how I had grown to love Ethiopia. The place that had terrified me just weeks earlier had become my dear friend. Home was beckoning me; yet, this place had made a home in my life that would never go away. Those two weeks had taught me to sing with all my heart, to give without holding back. I learned I can eat a lot of unusual foods and that I could be inspired by the very Christians I had come to teach. Perhaps what I learned most was that I am never alone. I may be mortified, overwhelmed and in complete fear ... but I am never alone. No child of God is ever alone.

I had found a peace like no other, as the little dark-faced children had pressed in around me. The swift beat of their songs still rang in my ears long after I had left the African continent. The smoky, outside aroma still hung onto my clothes after I opened my suitcase in my American home. The joy of thankful faces brought tears to my eyes. The memory of the ladies with the colorful skirts reminded me to believe; to believe not in myself, or the world around me, but in God and that His will is good.

Ethiopia taught me to love like I had never loved before. One day I would return to the land that had taught me so much. Until then, I would pray for those I had left behind and hold on to that African love. Love that came straight from the heart of God.

8

DISCOVERING PURPOSE

Growing Up

I could look back on the past several years and see progress and improvement in my growth and maturity ... especially spiritually. It was 2010. I was pleased with my life. I was 16 years old and successfully moving through high school as a homeschooler. The Lord had taught me over the past few years something of great importance, something that would change my thought process and life. God taught me that I had to make Him my God, that He just couldn't be my parents' God. I had to come to the point where I chose to serve Him because I believed Him, not just because my family or church did.

Quite honestly, I was very content. I was thankful for a wonderful home, family, church and life. Music had become a huge part of my life. I had taken piano for eight years and enjoyed using my skills in my church's praise team. I was by far the youngest singer and pianist our church had seen consecutively on stage. Yet, I didn't mind. I was honored.

The Lord had burrowed into my heart a passion that burned like a flame.

I was passionate about being a leader, even as a young teenager. I let Paul's words to young Timothy in 1 Timothy 4:12 be my guide, "Let no one despise you for your youth, but set the believers an example in speech, in conduct, in love, in faith, in purity."

There was no doubt that I had been in youth groups and had seen "teenagers." For the most part, I found a generation lacking in moral character. I was saddened by the number of churches who poured thousands of dollars into "youth activities," but I wondered what all of those activities did for those Christian teens. My sobering answer had to be: not much. I pondered what a crowd of immature 15-year-olds could teach another 15-year-old? Again, not much. Why were the adults pulling us off into a tie-dyed room with road signs on the walls and soft couches all around? All of the pizza, hot wings, go-karts and "innocent" lock-ins obviously taught my age group something, but what? By our actions, it was teaching us to be a needy, entitled and spiritually shallow bunch of kids.

After the trip to Ethiopia in 2009, I was disgusted by what I saw in America when I returned. In Africa the young adults struggled and worked. They begged to get to walk to church so they could sit in a stifling building and hear God's Word taught. They memorized an exorbitant amount of Bible verses so they could earn a Bible. Then there were a lot of us American Christians. We seem so complacent and content with our "fun" that we let the world around us slide away.

When the youth I knew turned 18 years old, most of them headed off to college. They smiled and promised to stay in touch and go to church. By the end of the first semester, most were gone. They abandoned all they had been taught. The world sucked them dry.

Their parents looked at my dad as the pastor and asked, "What happened?" Were the couple of hours at church every week not enough? Were the cute games and concerts not enough?

None of those things seemed wrong to me, but my question was, "Were those things enough?"

Not usually.

My parents poured into me and my siblings daily. They poured the Truth into our minds. The Truth is Jesus. It is the Bible. Because I was home schooled all of my school could be funneled through a Biblical worldview. They trained me to work. I hated it at first. Pulling weeds wasn't fun. Cleaning offices was boring and seemed demeaning. Having to figure out some of my problems on my own wasn't easy. Yet, I looked back and realized something. Those long, complicated studies of God's Word made me wiser. Serving my family as I cleaned and worked, made me more like Jesus. Saying "I am sorry" made me more humble. Maybe that was why my dad and mom did all of that.

My parents were my best friends and my hardest critics. They weren't perfect and neither did they have perfect children. However, they did a lot of things right. They showed me that they couldn't be my rock to lean on, but they wouldn't leave me weak and without a foundation. They gave me a foundation – Jesus Christ. They let Him be my Rock.

I can hear Daddy say these words after one of us children did something that pleased him, "I have no greater joy than to hear that my children are walking in the truth" (3 John 4).

Every part of my young heart had chosen to make my parent's faith my own. And that is what I saw missing in many other teenagers around me. They had been coddled and kept away from the "adults" for so long that by the time they were finally "allowed" into the services of their churches with the adults, they didn't want to be in the sanctuary where there wasn't nearly as much "excitement" or "fun." I can still hear some of my friends say, "Who would really want to go into those boring church services? They aren't any fun."

Mt. Pleasant Baptist Church began to implement youth activities in a whole new way. We were given roles in the church. We were called "young adults." We were raised to a place where we had a part in God's work. It worked. We still had fun, but it was a fun in accomplishing things for God's Kingdom. My dad even wrote a book about it entitled *Rite of Passage for the Home and Church: Raising Christ-Centered Young Adults*.

With my strong passion to see other young adults flourish in their walk with the Lord, I began an online blog. I expounded on my love for writing. I used my life as a way to bounce the Scripture out into the world. I in no way minded being on "display" for the world, in fact, I was used to it. My dad's job and calling as a pastor had constantly required me to be an example. Good or bad, I was an example.

Happily living life, I had placed Joshua Isaacs back into the deepest parts of my mind. I occasionally thought of how I would probably never see him again. I even wondered where he was every several months. To me, he was just another sad teenager who had left church with ambition to serve Jesus in college, and had lost that drive and never returned.

We Meet Again

My fingertips pushed against the rough guitar strings. The microphone stand in front of me picked up my voice and let the sound flow across the open field. The sweet scent of May lifted up with the freshly cut grass. A couple dozen church members opened up folding chairs and set up tables with hotdogs several yards away. My cousins, sister and I were singing for the evening worship. We were trying to get a quick practice in before everyone arrived. My peripheral vision saw Taylor bob her head to the lively beat of *I'll Fly Away*. The three-part harmony that met my ears made me smile. Kandace's violin hit her shoulder and she slid her bow effortlessly across the strings. I closed my eyes, enjoying the sun and music as we practiced. Suddenly, I heard a slight gasp from Kandace. I opened my eyes to see her surprised face as she nearly dropped her bow. I followed her gaze. It led a long distance away to a young man helping with a folding table. I squinted in the sunlight. I played the last chord of the song and stepped back from the microphone so my question wouldn't be heard by everyone.

"Who?"

Kandace may have answered, but I didn't hear her. The man turned to face me that very instant.

Josh.

It was without a doubt the man I thought I would never see again. His eyes met mine. Though one would possibly expect a sparkling, magical moment … that was not what happened. It was odd, really. I raised one eyebrow and cocked my head. My face must have asked the question I felt like yelling across field, "What are you doing here?" He smiled softly and turned away. Surprisingly, I felt no emotion at all, except for being intrigued. I laid my guitar down and went to help with the food as the locals in the community came out for the church function.

I was still trying to believe that Josh – long lost Josh – was there. I hadn't even known where he had spent the last few years. On such a small field, our paths crossed easily. So, I passed by him and I said something like, "Well, look who is back!" I felt bad after I said it. He just gave me a slight smile. It was on odd feeling. I almost felt sorry for him. He looked older and changed. He was still very attractive.

That was the first time I had seen Josh in a couple of years. No part of me believed that he would hang around. Josh was too much of a wanderer. He would be gone again in a few weeks or less than that. I wasn't trying to be judgmental. I was just wary. I was pleased that he was back, but that was all. I was just pleased. However, I didn't know how Josh felt. He told me years later that he was embarrassed and even scared to come back. He knew that many people had loved and supported him as he had gone to seminary, but he also knew that he had disappeared and let them down. They had a right to be disappointed.

Weeks did pass. Josh didn't leave. He was at church on Sundays and Wednesdays. He wanted to be involved. He didn't make his appearance really known, but he was back and he was consistent. Nothing was like it had been. The Katy who had been head-over-heels with infatuation with the cute and popular 17-year-old Josh was gone. I was a lot more mature. I had a lot more purpose. I was a musician and writer. Josh was just the guy who hadn't seemed to come to his full potential. I was right that Josh was wasting his days, but I was wrong to think that he would always be that way.

Becoming Friends

Acting had become one of my favorite passions. In 2009, I had seen a musical family called the Annie Moses Band perform in Winston-Salem, North Carolina. Their godly talent and love for music and fine arts inspired me. They hosted a camp every summer in Nashville, Tennessee for students to study music, dancing or drama. I was fascinated and drawn to this world of the arts. In my little corner of the world there were not many opportunities to use the arts for God's glory. It seemed that everything was about sports. I didn't hate sports. I enjoyed sports, but music and drama meant more to me. The Annie Moses Band offered what I had been longing for. They had opened up a world of music and arts. So, though the money was lacking, I begged Mama and Daddy for a chance to go to the Fine Arts Summer Academy (FASA). I recorded my voice and mailed a letter to the Annie Moses Band. A few weeks later, Mama told me that I had been given a partial scholarship. The remainder of the money could be taken care of.

I went to Nashville. The Annie Moses Band poured out extensive time and effort to make FASA an incredible experience. Those were two weeks of sheer bliss and the most beautiful music I had ever heard. There was a final show at the end of the camp. Every student dressed elegantly to perform the almost 3-hour long performance. It was bursting with music, drama and an orchestra of talented young adults. The music left me in tears. FASA became a part of my life. The following years, I went to FASA along with my younger sister Kandace and later, my little sister Clara. We saved money and cleaned business offices to make the extra money. It was worth it. Every penny.

My church started doing drama and we began to perform small skits during the services. My daddy was preaching about marriage for a few weeks in 2010. We pulled a few marriage skits together. I was assigned the part of the wife and we needed someone to play the husband. There wasn't a good candidate except Josh. Josh had been coming to church for a few months and everyone knew him, so I asked him. He accepted the part. I chuckled at the irony that he would play my husband after all the years I had begged God to let me marry him. I recall saying sarcastically, "Well, this is as close to marriage as Josh Isaacs and I are going to get!" We acted out the skits with ease. It was easy acting with Josh. We had fun and he was very good at drama. We played an oddly "good" husband and wife.

Josh became a new man. It was in those months that he truly determined to serve Jesus with his life. I was his constant friend, even when I found out that he was dating a girl from our church. I was burdened and confused by why he would date a girl that I truly believed he had no intention of marrying. Yet, Josh realized that God had a different plan for him and he moved on from that short relationship.

Just when I had become so comfortable with Josh's friendship in my life, he decided to join the Marines. Perhaps providentially, my parents played a role in encouraging Josh to join the military. Also, Josh was tired of having little purpose in his life and he wanted to do something that mattered. After praying about it and sensing God's direction, he went in with full speed. I was thrilled for him, yet I dreaded the day he would have to leave. And the day came sooner than either of us anticipated.

During the summer of 2011, while my family and I were in Nashville at the annual FASA, Daddy told us that Josh had been informed that he could leave for boot camp on July 25th. That would be the day that we would travel home from Nashville, but he would have to leave before we would get a chance to see him. I sent him an e-mail. I swallowed disappointment as I told him that I would miss him and would be praying for him. I would see him again in three months. Three months that would change our lives.

Boot Camp

The bus was the quietest place Josh found for a long time. A couple dozen other young men slept, temporarily unaware of the coming hours. Sleep was a gift that had never been so precious, but to Josh it seemed out of reach.

The bus lurched to a stop as the men piled out of the narrow stairs. A dirty, shadowy convenience store was across a small parking lot. One after another, the men purchased candy, drinks and snacks. Josh ignored the gnawing inclination that he should enjoy his last opportunity to indulge in junk food.

The bus door made a loud smacking sound after all of the men were back on. The serene, calmness erupted into a loud, gruff voice that seemed to shake the whole bus.

"Hold up your ID's!"

Josh fumbled for his ID at the hammering words. All the men held up cards. Behind the loud man loomed the gate. Stomachs flipped.

"Put your heads between your legs!" The man shouted.

Disorientation began to sink in. The privilege of looking out of the windows was over. With that first shocking realization that he was nothing and would be nothing to anyone behind that harsh gate, Josh's head started spinning. His mind screamed, *"I don't want to do this!"*

It seemed the bus would never stop. The veins in his head pounded as the blood rushed to his temples. He longed for and dreaded for the door to open.

The door opened.

"Get off of my bus! Get off of my bus!"

Tense bodies smashed into one another, clamoring to get off and terrified of the screaming instructor. Directly ahead were the dreaded, legendary footprints. The yellow footprints. There was no confusion as to what they must do. Several lines filled up. The instructor yelled, his hat shadowing his blazing eyes.

"Welcome to Parris Island!"

The shiny, metal doors ahead glimmered and proudly stated United States Marine Corps. Walking through the doors felt like walking into Hades. Paperwork was shuffled before his face. The last thing Josh wanted to do was sign his days, months and years away. Giving the Marine Corps freedom to do whatever they so pleased. Yet, his fingers scribbled Joshua C. Isaacs on every line to make the nightmare real.

Clothing and belongings were stripped away. Anything and everything held precious was removed. Each man was handed an identical mesh bag and mounds of gear and clothing were stuffed inside.

The first whole night dragged on with the extensive process of getting moved in. Over time, the locks of hair were roughly shaved from each head. Teeth were clenched as the blades unforgivingly scraped the skin.

Josh was ordered to stand against a wall, his head still burning. Dozens of others piled in. The bodies were so tightly packed that arms began to tingle with loss of blood flow as the sense of claustrophobia took hold.

The yelling hadn't ceased. Each new recruit was learning to be loud. Saying "me," "I," and "my" was out of line and punishable. Each shaven-headed recruit was a nobody and had to refer to himself as "this recruit."

Lines were formed as each recruit took a turn at an outdated payphone. Above the phone was a paragraph of curt, to-the-point words. They were the only words that could be spoken to the family member on the other end of the line. Constant clicks resounded as the phones snapped back in place after the recruits said, "I am here. I am well."

Everything was rigid. Josh sat cross-legged in a room lined with four rows of recruits. Their new rifles balanced between their legs. It became blatantly obvious that the waiting was training in itself. Hours would pass until recruits began to argue in harsh murmurs. Tension hung like a wet blanket over exhausted faces.

Eventually, drill instructors were assigned. Josh headed to the medical and dental area. When he thought he couldn't be dragged around anymore, he found himself in his squad bay. His permanent abode for three months. Although the word "abode" seemed a bit too cozy to appropriately describe the squeaky clean, bare-necessity barracks.

Josh's disdain for the temporary drill instructors fizzled away when the platoon's three permanent drill instructors marched in. The intensity of these three was unmatched.

Three randomly chosen recruits were ordered to run into the room. The drill instructors began to display their power by screaming into the faces of the recruits. Josh and the others watched quietly. The three recruits were quickly drenched in perspiration.

The instructors yelled exercise moves as rapidly as they could. The recruits were on the ground and back up again. Josh's mind tried to grasp the point.

Would this be the kind of workout they would receive as a punishment?

He had been very active as a child, especially in high school. Flashbacks of running track flittered through his mind. The football coaches pushing him and the sticky wrestling mat as he pinned down yet another opponent. But this training. This was crazier than anything he had seen.

The instructors turned to face the silent recruits.

"If you do not understand and do not follow through with our instructions, you will do as these recruits have shown you."

Silence.

"Do you understand?!"

"Yes, sir!" The sound reverberated off of the walls.

Choosing to Stay

The first month was bombarded with the details of how to behave. Constant drilling went hand in hand. The recruits learned exactly how to eat, walk and even breathe all over again. They experienced that a meal was not meant to be a break in the action, but the time allotted was generally just a few minutes … or seconds.

Weakness and aches spread like wildfire. Josh traced the earliest feelings of sickness back to the half-dozen immunization shots he had received in one day.

Dental was the scariest place of all. With his mouth stretched open, the brash hygienists claimed, "They must come out." So three wisdom teeth were removed. Lying awake, Josh forced himself to ignore the ripping, tugging sensation. When it was all over, there were no milkshakes and comfortable pillows. There was lukewarm water and push-ups.

If that wasn't miserable enough, Josh developed a respiratory infection that left him wheezing and cringing with a raw throat. Every ounce of strength he had ever possessed was being tested. Mutilated.

The moment of truth awaited him at the doctor. It was his second trip there because of this sickness and nothing was helping.

"Look," said the nurse. "We can't do anything else to help you. You have two choices …"

Josh swallowed hard. He knew what those choices were.

"Leave or tough it out."

This was his chance. He had his excuse to get out. This misery could be over. Yet, there was suddenly a myriad of images that flooded his cluttered brain. Church, family, friends, and his faithful mentor, Kevin. They were counting on him. He couldn't just quit. But he knew that he had to move on from his obsessive hatred of the place. Choose. Move on. Leave. Excuses. Integrity.

His own ears were surprised by his confident voice. "I will stay."

Overcoming

Letters! The drill instructor held a wad of envelopes in his hand. The recruits reminded themselves to seem relaxed. Names were shouted as the envelopes flew through the air like confetti. The recruits were allowed to scour the floor, searching for their letters. Josh smiled as he spotted his name. It was beyond refreshing to see his name, carefully and lovingly printed. A letter from Kevin, one from the Bible Study, one from his mom and one from Kathryn Brown. A smile crossed his face at the sight of the last letter.

His sparse moments each day of down time were easily filled with reading letters, reading the Bible and praying. Each letter brought him peace and joy like a soaking rain on a cracked and dry ground. He couldn't help but notice one of the other recruits never had a letter to pick up off of the ground. He always sat by as every other man tore through his envelopes. Josh handed him a few of his own letters and shared news from the outside world, hoping it would bring the guy some sort of comfort.

My letters to Josh were a few pieces of college-ruled notebook paper with random information about church, the weather, Bible verses and reminders that he would get through the days ahead. Those letters weren't superior or beautifully written, but they were his favorites. The letters of others were placed in the wooden box at the foot of his bed. But mine, were often held close and even on occasion, they were placed under his pillow at night. He wasn't sure why the words of a 17-year-old girl made him feel the way he did yet, he knew that regardless of the reason, he wanted me close by and he missed me.

Sundays were joyful. At least the mornings were pleasant. Almost everyone went to chapel. At chapel there was a rare gift … music. Josh quickly came to love the song "At the Foot of the Cross" by Kathryn Scott. It reminded him of church services back at home. The next opportunity he had, he scribbled Kathryn Brown on an envelope and wrote on a piece of paper, "I love this song. Have you heard it?"

When I received his letter, I carried it with me everywhere. Like Josh, I was unsure why I loved his letters. I just knew that I loved them. Somehow, I was certain that those letters were helping him and me. They were plain, simple, friendly, but so much more powerful than anyone knew.

"Yes!" I replied. "I have heard it!"

I plopped down on the piano bench that day and learned that song. I sang the words and played the notes until they were smooth and beautiful. I promised myself that one day I would play it for him.

Anger's Punishment

The scrub brush went back and forth in a tight, rhythmic motion on a heavy weight. Josh bent over, forcing his shoulder to maintain the weight's balance midair – just inches from the floor. Frustration and pain coiled through his core. Josh switched hands quickly to give the other one in agony a break.

Walker, the recruit just a few feet over, wasn't too happy that Josh had switched hands. So he shoved Josh roughly. His firm grip on the weight wavered with the jolt. Without thinking, Josh pushed him back. It was meant to relay a clear message: Leave me alone and mind your own business. Assuming he had the last push, Josh turned back as a pounding blow sent the world around him into blackness.

Josh's eyelids peeled apart, accompanied by splintering pain. The senior drill instructor leaned over. A slight emotion of concern etched his hard features.

"What happened?" He snapped.

Josh struggled to shout out what had occurred.

"… and hit this recruit, sir!"

Warm blood trickled as he stood to his feet. It felt like tears streaming down his cheek. The senior drill instructor's short, muscular body forcefully led Josh to the restroom where they attempted to wash the wounds. It was clear that he would need stitches.

The third instructor – known as the Kill Hat – was known for torturing or "killing" the recruits in workouts, but he was ironically the one who took Josh to the hospital. It was under terrible circumstances that one calls a basic training hospital a piece of heaven. But "heaven" was Josh's word to describe the cool, clean interiors of the medical building. Sweet nurses gently called him "honey" and "sugar" as they examined his wounds.

Munching on peanut butter crackers and noisily slurping two cold juice-boxes, Josh listened like a child as a nurse explained that he had a scull fracture and that it would hopefully heal correctly on its own.

After two stitches under his eye, two stitches on the back of his head and one above his eyebrow, he was free to go. Free to leave the heavenly place with pixie voices, cold drinks, gentle hands and no drill instructors. *Free to go back to bondage.*

The Kill Hat was rather funny and joked good-naturedly on the way back to the rest of the platoon. Josh decided that the tall, gangly "killer" was his favorite instructor.

Josh's face remained swollen and sore for days. The skull fracture ached with the workouts. However, the pain didn't match or compete with the humiliation of all three drill instructors singling him out shortly after the ordeal and making fun of him in front of all of the recruits. They pointed and bellowed loud jokes into his disfigured face. Talking back was never an option, but the anger and hurt burned like a hot skillet on cool skin. Josh held his tongue because it was his only option at the time, but he learned that keeping silent when fury raged was a lesson he could have benefited from long ago in his life. He was learning valuable lessons there, even if the place's teaching techniques were extreme.

Home Stretch

Days turned into weeks. As time passed, Josh learned how to get through the excruciating workouts without losing focus. Other recruits were pushed further back into their stay on Parris Island because of injuries and depression. Josh determined that he wanted off the island and the quickest way off was to graduate. He felt his body's broken exhaustion slowly turn the corner toward extremely incredible strength. He easily took to shooting his rifle and came up as an expert shooter. Joy was like a fountain when he slipped his last letter into an envelope. It was full of anticipant information about the Family Day and Graduation Day to take place on the 20th and 21st of October.

The last and most difficult challenge awaited Josh on a dark morning only a few days before his graduation.

The Crucible.

Josh later had difficulty describing the intensity of The Crucible to its true nature. The Crucible was fifty-four hours long, but felt like an eternity. It began with a long hike. Food and sleep deprivation highlighted the innermost struggles of the rigorous mental obstacles. The forty-five miles of marching left one's legs numb and combat assault courses left one jittery. Josh maneuvered through wires and over wooden courses. The recruits had to focus on each other and work as a team. The dark woods were so dense that the mind started to deceive and envision things that were not there. Dirt and filth accumulated on their gear and skin. It rained enough to soak through the layers of clothing and left the recruits damp and clammy.

Getting through each hour took focusing on the finish line. It was a matter of saying, "almost done" and leaning for the end with one last lung full of air. Marching back after it was all over was jubilance. Though exhaustion had never been more prevalent, there was a vibe of accomplishment and pride.

While my family made our way to Charleston, South Carolina to enjoy a few days of vacation prior to Josh's Family Day and Graduation Day, Josh thrilled in the famed "Eagle, Globe and Anchor Ceremony." It was a sacred moment after The Crucible when the recruits were officially recognized as marines. The drill instructors firmly placed the emblem in each marine's palm. Eyes met as the sealed promise was granted. Josh relished a "Warrior's Breakfast," where he ate heartily.

Josh had finished boot camp. He would graduate in a few days, but the work was over. Little did he know that with an emblem in his palm, he would be entering a whole new world that would change his life in more ways than he could have imagined. Basic Training may have been designed to build a stronger man, but Josh was more than just a stronger man; he was a new man. A bright future lay at his feet, stretching for miles. Josh had fought for every inch of it.

9
LOVE'S OPENING LINES

A New Man

My family drove onto the marshy island that bright morning of Family Day. I was shaking with excitement to see Josh. I had imagined and re-imagined every moment of that day. I wore a dark blue shirt, proudly supporting the 3rd Battalion. The anticipation climbed like a roller coaster car pulling up a hill. The morning was cold as we waited in line to go into the large gymnasium-like building. Our family sat watching time tick. We had not managed to find Josh's family. His mom, aunts and grandmother were there along with the Jeffcoat family. The Jeffcoats were the family Josh had worked for and lived with for a time in his late teens. Eric Jeffcoat and my dad had made a point to come to the graduation since Josh's father wouldn't be present.

Finally, a few drill instructors shouted some words. Music rang as one platoon after another marched in from the side of the building. The national anthem reverberated as the flag of the United States of America was held high and proud. Josh said that his heart felt like it would explode as he watched the large door lift to the ceiling, bidding them to enter. Their perfect, synchronized marching left the crowd in reverent awe. When I didn't think I could take waiting another second, I heard the words, "The senior drill instructors will now dismiss their platoons."

With one short sentence, the marines broke into freedom. I watched families erupt out of their seats and fall into their son's, husband's and father's arms. I looked for Josh's face, my dream of running into his arms playing in my mind. Daddy led us into the middle of the people. There was no sign of Josh. I cringed, wondering how long it would take us to find him. Daddy suggested that we go wait outside. As we walked toward the door, I saw him; and this sight was like nothing I had imagined. There he stood and he was so handsome. Yet, it was his heart that I saw shortly after. His will had not been broken by this place, but it had been channeled into an intentional outlet. His personality and passion had been pushed and prodded to make him a man of great purpose.

Daddy swung around and saw him. Daddy just about ripped him off of the ground into a bear hug. Josh smiled as he hugged Mama and waved at Kandace, Clara and Andrew. My plans collapsed as he looked at me. He smiled right into my eyes as though he could touch my very soul. It was like the little sparklers Mama used to give us on the Fourth of July. When one's sparkler was lit, all it took was a second or two pressed against another sparkler to light it's sizzling flame. That one glance was Josh's sparkler lighting mine. The clear blue purity of his eyes sent my heart sizzling with a feeling I knew nothing about.

Josh's family stood around him jabbering and chatting. We left the building and spent the morning touring around Parris Island. Josh led us and even stopped traffic so we could peacefully cross the streets. His actions confirmed my thought.

He is a new man.

Josh told me months later that God taught him one truth above many truths. God had allowed the Marine Basic Training to unknowingly convey this message from Him:

When I am all you have, I am all you need.

It revolutionized his life.

Josh and I didn't talk much that first day, but the letters between us were reread in my mind. I just smiled into his eyes and he did the same to me.

The next morning was so chilly that my blue jean jacket felt like it was nonexistent. I shivered on the cold bleacher. After hundreds of new marines had marched across the wide concrete expanse, they completed their graduation. I nearly dropped the camcorder with happiness. This time it didn't take forever to find him. I made a beeline straight for Josh. I hugged him tightly as I whispered, "I'm so proud of you." He looked into my eyes. His sharp uniform beautifully silhouetted against the blue sky.

Suddenly, it was all over. I'm not sure how it happened or what made the time go by so quickly, but we were saying goodbye and getting in the van to go home. Josh happily reminded us that he would see us on Sunday. I was pleased as I remembered that he would be home for ten days.

When I was finally back in my room in my house, I sat on my bed and gripped the letters Josh had sent me over the past few months. It was all over. The long wait was over. I felt old. I felt withered. Knowing that the Graduation Day was coming had helped propel me forward. I had been looking forward to that day for reasons I didn't understand myself. As I marked through the Graduation Day on my faithful calendar, I realized that Josh would be leaving. Ten days would fly by and he would be gone again. This time it would be for forever.

A Song and A Hayride

Maybe it was providence that allowed me to have the Sunday after Josh got home to play a song at church. That particular Sunday I could do any song I wanted, so I chose "At the Foot of the Cross" (the song he had sent me months earlier). I played it and sang the lyrics, hoping it would make Josh smile and more importantly, make Jesus smile. The ending of the song was smoothly retarding when I went to play the last "E chord" and accidently omitted the "A sharp," creating a horrible "E minor" to end the song. I felt my face flush. But afterward, Josh came up to me and with a look of honesty, he said, "It was beautiful, Kathryn. Beautiful."

The following day, we had Josh over for supper. After a delicious meal of chicken and dumplings and relaxed conversation,

Daddy took us to Bible Study. He enjoyed getting to celebrate and fellowship with old friends. I looked into Josh's face and it hit me once again that he was a new man. He was serious and purpose-driven. I was amazed. He was turning into the kind of man I wanted to marry.

On Wednesday, there was a Fall Festival at church. Josh had nothing to do so he came and helped run one of the games. Little kids squealed and played as Josh and I worked. After a while, I walked up to Josh and said, "I think I may go outside and ride on the hayride. I just wanted to let you know."

I hoped he might follow me. Within mere seconds, he had retired from his duties and ran up behind me. "May I go with you?"

I nodded. As we climbed onto the old tractor covered in sweet-smelling hay, I reminded myself that others were watching. I also reminded myself that I couldn't just fall "head-over-heels" with Josh again. So we sat there. The cold wind whipping at my hair, I enjoyed the moment.

"Kathryn, this world would be a better place if we were all as mature and sweet as you."

I saw something in his eyes that I hadn't seen before. The distant lights of the church fell upon his face as the lumbering hayride turned the corner. I wrote in my journal that night:

October 27, 2011

I sat on the hayride thinking, I better soak it in because he is leaving forever. I almost cried. He told me about how my Dad had told him that he would probably never see him for more than a day or two a year. Josh said that he doesn't want that to happen. He said that he didn't care if he ever came back to Wilkes County when he first went to Basic Training, but he said that now he doesn't feel that way anymore.

For the first time, I had Josh all to myself. He called me Kathryn and it was perfect. It was then that it hit me.

Do I still have feelings for him?

I lay here crying as I write these words. I'm not trying to be dramatic. I have never loved any man except for Josh. I can't lie about it.

I don't know what he thinks about me. All I know is that I love him and I want him to live the amazing life God has for him.

I simply prayed tonight that if Josh is not the one for me that God would take this love away and if he is … I pray that the love will stay no matter what. If he is the one, then I will wait all four years for him until he is out of the Marines. Yet, if he is not the one then I pray that God will bring him the right woman.

I need God to show me if it is okay for me to feel this way. If it isn't then He will help me overcome this, because it would not be fair for me to love another woman's future husband. But there is one thing Josh will always be … he will always be my brother.

Making the Days Count

A few years earlier, I had decided that I wouldn't date. It wasn't something that was forced upon me by my parents. I watched other young adults and even teenagers, who were hardly more than children, as they dated. Seeing what "dating" did to many of them left a bitter taste in my mouth.

Dating allowed so much freedom and that freedom turned to danger. A girl and a boy would go out together and no one really knew why. It was just supposed to be fun. Over time that boy and girl would get very attached. They would be in each other's company … often times they would be alone. Some parents would tell their children to "be careful." But that seemed like telling gasoline and fire not to explode when they are right beside each other. It seemed very hard to stay pure when in that sort of a relationship. Friends of mine dated and I was amazed by the way their very personalities tended to change. Their hearts became entangled in this giddy, pleasant relationship. Over time, many broke up with their childhood sweethearts. Their hearts were calloused and torn apart. High school came and went, and often times, so did their purity. If you weren't dating, then you weren't popular. For some, they really believed they loved their boyfriend or girlfriend and then college hit. The tide of life swept through and the "love" they thought they shared, washed away.

When my daddy was still the youth pastor at church, teenage girls would come to him, crying because they had broken up with their boyfriends. "Broken-hearted" was the word. Like a paper heart ripped to shreds. It didn't have to be that way. Even I had an idea of that broken-hearted pain. I had experienced it only a few years earlier when I became overwhelmed and completely consumed with an immature infatuation with Josh. The Bible had a much better plan for the way love should unfold. Dating was a product of wealthy families in the 1950s. America boomed after WWII and parents bought their children cars. Off they went to movies and various other hangout spots. Dating was born.

What should the intention of dating be in the first place? I wondered and realized that the only reason a young man and a young woman should be spending time together in that way was to seek marriage. Yet, that wasn't what the youth I knew were doing. They were just having a good time. Maybe "just having a good time" was never God's intent. In the Bible, people were betrothed. It is a heavy word, but that was the word used to describe Mary and Joseph's relationship in the second chapter of Luke. Betrothal was so permanent that breaking it required a certificate of divorce. In the Bible, the process leading up to marriage was a serious thing. It wasn't as cheap and easy as dating.

Courtship is somewhere between betrothal and dating. When I thought of courtship, I imagined a little parlor in a late 19th century home. Country time blue, with bright yellow coming through the wavy glass windows as a pretty woman sits straight with a slight smile. A handsome gentleman in a fine suit sits across the room, looking dazzlingly in love. They chat happily and dream of being married one day with a parlor like this of their very own.

Courting and Betrothal. Betrothal and Courting. Either way I sliced it, both were more pure, accountable, and worthwhile than dating. Both led to marriage. I knew with all of my heart I didn't want a broken heart. I wanted to wear a white dress on my wedding day and be able to know that I was pure. I wanted something deeper and stronger than what the American culture had to offer.

I knew that if God could create me and make me His child, then surely He could bring to me the man I would marry. I just needed to wait. Waiting would relieve me from the burden of having to "go looking" for a man. God knew him before I even existed. God would bring him.

Little did I know, I would soon have to determine whether I was really going to follow through with the covenant I had made years earlier. I wouldn't have months or years to choose my path … I would have moments – seconds to distinguish the path I would take.

The Gloves

Saturday I awoke before the sun had peeked over the mountains. It was blustery morning as a sweet, young couple picked me up so we could go hand out clothes and food to the homeless in the inner city Winston-Salem, North Carolina. Jason and Katie Church were quickly becoming some of my dearest friends. They would later feel the Lord's call to sell everything and move 1,200 miles to the southern tip of Texas to a city called Weslaco, where they would serve as a missionary couple. They would work across the border in Progreso, Mexico and in Weslaco to share the Gospel with many who had never even heard about Jesus and His saving grace.

I happily hopped in their car and we were off to pick up Josh and then another friend named Ashley Pendry. We laughed and talked all the way to Winston and huddled close as we handed out warm clothes to the shivering men, women and children. It felt good to be with friends. We sang a few songs and Josh requested that I sing some of his favorite songs from church. He smiled as I sang.

We were all eating lunch together afterward when Katie piped, "You two should come with us to go see the football game up at Appalachian!" If any of my friends knew anything about me, they knew that I didn't just love football. I also didn't just love freezing half to death while I watched a football game. Whether Josh wanted to watch football, hang out with friends or both, I didn't know, but he grinned a little too widely and said, "I'd love to!"

I wanted to go because Josh was going, but I wouldn't act so easily persuaded.

"Ah, I don't know," I said. "I should call Daddy and ask if I may go."

I did and Daddy said yes. But Josh didn't know that, so while I was on the phone he touched my arm and offered, "I'll pay for your ticket."

I chuckled inwardly. "No thank you, Josh. Daddy said I could go though."

Boone, North Carolina – the home of Appalachian State University – was where both my mama and daddy went to college. It loomed above my foothill home about thirty minutes up the beautiful mountain, which crawls with tourists each fall as the trees turn vibrant shades.

The stadium was bursting with people. There were so many bodies that I became genuinely concerned that I would get lost. I grabbed the back of Josh's shirt as Jason and Katie plowed through the masses. He turned his head.

"Don't let me get lost!" I joked.

His face surely didn't mean to become so somber. "I would never let you get lost, Kathryn."

Sitting in the damp, muddy grass because there were no more seats, Josh found a piece of cardboard for me to sit on so my pants wouldn't get wet. I had on leather gloves and a warm coat, yet the frozen air was causing my fingers to tingle and turn numb. Josh felt of my fingers at my request and suddenly disappeared up the steep hill. He came down a while later with a pair of warm, black gloves. He had a silly toboggan on his head and identical gloves on his hands. He held out the gloves.

My mouth fell open. "You didn't have to do that!"

"Kathryn, I couldn't let you freeze."

I gratefully said "thank you" and slid them onto my icy fingers, letting my elevated heartbeat pound the words in my mind: he takes care of me.

After a long game, which I cared little about, we loaded our cold selves into Jason and Katie's car. Ashley had met up with her boyfriend, Robby.

On the way down the mountains, Josh talked about Boot Camp. We asked him what he would be doing from then on. After a while of chatter, he let his eyes drop to stare into his lap as he said that he wished he could take all of us with him.

Katie was always one to say what she was thinking. "Well, Jason and I can't go with you, but Katy could!" She laughed and then said a little too seriously, "You would just have to marry her first."

I completely expected Josh to laugh and roll his eyes. He didn't. "I couldn't marry her yet anyways. She is only 17-years-old." *Does that mean he has actually considered marrying me?*

The Hardest Goodbye of My Life

Sunday came. Josh spent a lot of time with me. The church held a Resolution Signing. The men of the church participated in a ceremony, committing to be godly men. Josh was thrilled to get to be involved. He signed his name on a fancy certificate. It was all symbolic as dozens of men came and stood at the front of the church for a group photo. That photo would later be hung in the foyer of the church.

It was beginning to sink in as I sat across from him at the table that Sunday night. The very real and burdensome fact that he was leaving the next day took hold of my very core.

The night was over. I asked Josh if he would be at Bible Study the next night. He said that he thought so, but he would have to leave right after that. I nodded, happy and sad. I longed for just a moment to talk with him like I had on that hayride. I wanted just a few minutes to have his undivided attention and to tell him that I would always be there for him. Yet, I knew that such a treasured moment would not come.

The next day was Halloween. I still say that Halloween 2011 was one of the most upsetting days of my young life. After a wonderful Bible Study at Jason and Katie's house, we all headed outside to roast marshmallows. Josh tried to show off as he bent old wire-hangers into long sticks to put the marshmallows on. With a crackling fire, Christian radio playing and dear friends all around, it seemed that I had no right to be as down as I was.

In the midst of the chatter, Josh made one of the most heart wrenching comments.

"After this I probably won't be able to come home for a year or more. I just don't know when I'll get extended leave again."

I stared into the fire, feeling a disappointment that I had only heard about. My throat closed with tears. Turning my head, I saw the dark woods behind me. The light of the fire only carried so far; behind me ran the cold darkness for miles.

I just want to wander into those woods and never come back.

As horrible a thought as it may have been, I still thought it.

That was the beginning of the long, hard night. Everyone started to leave. I knew that someone had dropped Josh off and I wasn't sure how he would get home. The awkward tension grew until I decided that I had to leave. Josh asked quietly if I could drop him off since he was living only a mile down the road. I agreed, wondering how I would handle any more tension.

Driving away, the windshield on my car started to fog up. I hadn't been driving for many months and in the time I had been running the roads I hadn't enjoyed driving. I tried to remain calm as the glass turned foggy.

"You want to turn on your defrost?" Josh asked.

"Yeah, well, I'm not really sure how to do that!" I embarrassingly laughed.

He hit the defrost button and the windshield cleared up. For some odd reason, I almost burst into tears.

What am I going to do without him?

It was way too soon for it all to be ending as I pulled into the driveway. Complete sickness and dread filled my insides like poison. I stopped the car and looked at him, the faint interior car light casting an eerie shadow.

"Well, thanks for bringing me home." Each word seemed to take all of his strength to mutter.

I wanted to die as he reached for the door handle.

Is this it? All of my heart's aching for this abrupt ending?

"Josh," I said as I laid my hand on his shoulder. "Please, keep in touch."

"Of course, yeah." He opened the door and stood up. A suppressed pain was on his face. "I'll see you, Kathryn."

He was gone. I sat there in my car. I wanted to get out and run to his door and shout, "this can't be it!" I wanted to do something to make the painful misery in my heart go away, but there was nothing to do. I fumbled the car into "reverse" and backed out. I don't remember how I even got home. That five-minute drive home was one of the very darkest moments of my life.

He is gone and he will never be back. You chose to love the wrong person.

The road blurred as tears rolled down my cheeks. I didn't want to go home. I didn't want to face my family. It was all I could do to pray – to beg God for the strength to face each moment ahead. I didn't fully understand what was wrong with me.

Why would leaving Josh hurt so much? What had happened to me to bring me to this point? What had I done?

I opened the door to my house and dropped my keys on the table. Mom and Dad asked how everything had been. I lied and said that all was well. They must have known something wasn't right. Everything about the way I acted was forced and fake.

Everyone went to bed and I sat on my bed in my room. My mind wandered back to over five years before when I had "loved" Josh. I had been so confused and embarrassed. I had decided not to date since then and I know that I had matured. I tried to distinguish whether this time was different. I quickly realized that it was very different. This time I wasn't embarrassed. This time it felt right, not wrong. This time I wanted the best for him and not just the best for myself. This time I needed someone to know. I felt a "knowing" that the fact that Josh and I were apart was wrong. I belonged with him. It made no sense, but I knew that I couldn't hold the emotions to myself any longer.

Mom and Dad's room seemed like a welcomed refuge as I knocked on the doorframe. Daddy looked up from the rocking chair and asked what I was still doing up. From there everything exploded out of me. I broke down as the childish-sounding words came out of my mouth, "I'm going to miss him so much!"

Daddy and Mama made eye contact. Mama's face seemed to say, "I told you" to Daddy's astonished one. Between my sharp intakes of breath, I told them that I just didn't know what to do.

"Honey." Daddy's voice was sweet but firm. He hugged me. "I understand, I do, but you need to understand that Josh is gone."

I fought the urge to back out of his arms.

Mama then chimed in. "You have spent a lot of time with him the last few days. I believe that over time you will think of him less. Just pray that God will help you move on."

Daddy spoke next. "I love Josh, Kate. But you need to understand that he is really not who I had in mind for you. I just imagine a different kind of man … with a different background and life. He is gone and he may be back every once in a while, but certainly not often. You can't live waiting for him to come around."

Since I had unloaded all of my burdens at their feet, I wasn't ready or receptive to the words my parents were saying. They were good and true, but still hard to hear.

"Daddy, I know all of that. I know that he isn't what you and Mama always imagined for me. I have tried so hard to keep my heart pure for the man I will marry, but I'm so drawn to Josh. I don't know why. I know all of the things from his past that he carries, but I … I don't even know what he feels. Maybe nothing at all …."

"Pray about it," was their response.

That was something I could do.

I went to bed with the gloves Josh had bought for me at the football game. I held them under my pillow as I prayed for this man who kept reentering and then leaving my life. I prayed that God would bring him back to me, or help me let him go for good.

10

STRONGER THAN SEPARATION

Placing it in His Hands

November 2, 2011
I will have to get to the point where I can love him without crying constantly. It will have to be put on hold. It won't mean that I don't love him, but that I'm waiting, just waiting.

The first few days after Josh left I cried more than I cared to admit. I prayed that Josh would figure out a way to get home for Christmas. It was a lofty dream, but I clung to it. Josh was busy in more training. He spent his days in dark forests in more intense outside training. The cold, wet, primitive conditions were a new type of training. His cell phone was taken for the majority of his time there. Each marine only had a few moments to call on one rare occasion. Josh immediately called my daddy's cell phone. I heard Daddy answer, "Josh! Hey!"

I was stunned that he was on the phone. I was shaking with joy. Just to hear his voice. I motioned for Daddy to put his voice on speakerphone so we could all hear him. Tears gathered in my eyes at the sound of his voice. I never said anything to Josh over the phone that day even though we both wished later that I had. But hearing his voice at all was more than I could have dreamed. It made me smile for many days following.

Life became busy as I planned and packed for my second trip to Ethiopia. This trip, my 13-year-old sister, Kandace would be going with us. We geared our minds for the trip. I prayed that God would keep sickness away from us this time. I was nervous and excited. Mission trips have always given me such feelings of anticipation. I knew that 10 villages in the heart of Africa awaited me. I had much to share with the many children I would meet. With the plethora of emotions and burdens I was carrying, I struggled in the days prior to leaving.

November 13, 2011
I went to the altar today. I usually am singing so I can't go down, but it felt good to literally fall before the throne. When I got there I felt like I was in water. I weighed nothing ... I just cried, about Ethiopia, Josh, and life. You know what? It felt wonderful. I could only whisper "You're enough." And I believed it. Am I scared about the trip? Yes. Am I worried about Josh and if he cares for me? Yes. Will I let all of that run me? No. It is in His hands. Thank God.

Return to Africa

It was a bright Wednesday morning when we met the rest of the mission team at the airport. There was a long flight and a layover in Amsterdam, Holland. We flew to the Sudan for another short layover and finally landed in Addis Ababa, Ethiopia for the second time in my life. The smoky smell rolled over us as soon as our feet hit the ground. It honestly caused me to panic for an instant. I was thankful that over the two years that Ethiopia and I had been apart, God had strengthened me to be less fearful of what was ahead. Kandace, on the other hand, was less sure as she lugged her suitcase into the guesthouse. I promised her that it seemed scarier than it was and that everything would be perfectly fine, but the stress and exhaustion ran her over like a boulder and she cried softly to herself.

The next morning we ate a hearty breakfast and prepared to make the familiar 6-hour drive to Alaba. In 2009, we had ridden to Alaba in an old bus, but this year we took the Land Cruiser. It was faster, smaller and easier to weave through traffic. On the way to Alaba we were packed on top of each other as we zipped down the road. Daddy tried to remain calm, but even he closed his eyes as we passed cars with fast, oncoming traffic zooming toward us. The stunning African sunset silhouetted the vehicle as we arrived in front of dear Marta and Demessie's house. I laughed and smiled as I greeted old friends.

The first day was very pleasant as we relaxed and prepared for the week. Daddy, Kandace and I slept in two adjoining rooms. Kandace and I shared a bed and Daddy had his own twin-sized bed. Kandace found that the food was certainly different from anything she had ever eaten, which was a lesson Dad and I had learned on our first trip. We said a thankful prayer for a good day and headed to bed. The recorded Muslim "crier" in a nearby mosque eerily resounded over loudspeakers. The haunting cry made me shudder. We were told that the Muslim crier went on longer on Saturday nights, because they knew that Christians would get up and go to church the next morning. The sad, hopeless sound rang in our ears as we fell asleep.

The Suitcase Bed

I awoke to Kandace yelling weakly, "Daddy, Daddy! I need a bowl!" I was wondering if I was dreaming or awake when Dad put a bowl below Kandace's face as she vomited. I sat up, feeling the heat radiating off of her clammy body.

Not again.

I was dumfounded, wondering how she could be sick. She must have felt the same way as she moaned, "Daddy, why am I sick? Why?"

Daddy, always trying to be optimistic, patted her head with a damp cloth. "Maybe it's just a short thing."

I jumped out of the bed and changed clothes, hoping to rid myself of any germs. I glanced at the clock, expecting to see that it was 4:00 a.m. or even later.

11:30 p.m.

Kandace fell back asleep and Daddy allowed me to join him on his twin-sized bed. The little black ants and wooly sheets were highly uncomfortable. I gave myself permission to cry and I did so until I fell asleep. A few hours later Kandace was vomiting again. I bolted out the door into the cool night air. I could hear Daddy comforting her. I glared in to the sky and I watched the stars twinkle. I was reliving the 2009 trip.

God, why does this have to happen? Are we all going to get sick? Is she going to stay sick for days? Please make her better!

Once I walked back inside, Kandace was dozing back off to sleep and Daddy was on his bed. I knew that Daddy had to preach to over 2,500 people at church the following morning, so he desperately needed his sleep and another body in his tiny bed was not conducive for that. For the second time in my life, I pulled two suitcases together and laid towels and clothes over them. I laid down on my makeshift bed, just as I had done over two years before and fell asleep.

The next day, Kandace was weak but she was recovering. Daddy went to preach while I stayed in the room to watch after her. I was disappointed that I couldn't go to church, but I knew that she needed me. Her fever lingered over 99 degrees most of the day. Later that night, the team gathered to video message the church back at home. With the seven-hour time difference, we could Skype the church and the technical guys at church would put the video on the large screens during the service. It was exciting and surreal to get to speak to the entire church from 7,000 miles away. Kandace was even well enough to come and be a part.

The following days were wonderful. Kandace came out of her sickness with a new outlook and appreciation for health. Some have asked my parents why they would allow their children to go on mission trips considering the challenges they must inevitably face. My parents chose to let us experience different countries and serve in mission work because of the command in Acts 1:8 that says, "But you will receive power when the Holy Spirit has come upon you, and you will be my witnesses in Jerusalem and in all Judea and Samaria, and to the ends of the earth." I learned early on that children aren't excluded from that mandate.

If I am a disciple of Jesus, then I am to be a witness, whether I am eight years old or 80 years old. Being a witness as a child broadened my view of true Christianity. It forced me to look outside of myself and taught me to overcome the strong urge to fulfill only my personal wants and needs. It is a disease that many Christians seem to have succumbed – the disease of selfishness. It was clear to me that everyone, including the very strongest Christians, deal with the heavy burden of selfishness, but how much it consumes a person is completely up to them. Mission work is like a dam in the river of selfishness. It holds it back.

The Blessing of Serving

Our team split up that week as we served the people. Our group consisted of seven members. A lady from Dr. and Mrs. Black's church, Bethel Hill Baptist in Roxboro, North Carolina, had joined us in Ethiopia along with her daughter. Cindi and Abigail Jacobs were a fun duet. Cindi was a veteran of the work in Ethiopia. She spent the weeks teaching the women in the villages. Abigail helped Kandace and me as we taught the children in the villages. Relaxed and faithful, Ethiopia veteran Jason Hatley was also from Bethel Hill. He taught the men in Bible Studies. Dale Jennings had been on the trip with me in 2009 and had traveled back with my dad in 2010. He has always been the example of a true, unbending disciple of Christ. He taught the men in villages and in the prison nearby. My daddy taught in the Alaba "mother church." They called it the mother church because from that church had come 23 other churches in the surrounding villages.

My heart nearly exploded with joy as the children burst out of the weeds and thickets as the Land Cruiser passed by. They jumped and shouted as we joined them. Their eyes shimmered with the thrill of understanding as we acted out the dramatic, Biblical stories. I didn't want to leave the people. I hugged the little warm bodies and soaked in the image of huts and colorful cloth against the blue sky. I breathed the earthy smell. The children's dirty hands gripped mine and I held them close. This place was hard. The work visibly wore on the natives, but these people reminded me that life is sweet ... even when it is so very difficult.

After the trips out to the dusty villages, we were covered in a thin layer of dirt. Mercy (one of the daughters of Marta and Demessie) knocked on our door a few days into the trip.

"Water warm for Keety and Kandace," her soft voice spoke to my dad.

I had never been so thankful for a large bucket of warm water. The bucket was placed in the bathroom (the little box like structure with a hole in the ground). It stunk and there were countless bugs, so one had to quickly wash off and keep the water pouring over the skin so that the bugs would stay off. Yet, it was glorious and I thanked Jesus for warm water. I thanked Him for Mercy. Her name suited her, I thought.

I had only begun to see the surface of what the Christians in Ethiopia experienced. I had experienced it two years before, but this time my more mature mindset really grasped the intensity of life.

Then we met Oshe. I had heard about Oshe for a few years. He lived in the southern mountains of Ethiopia, burrowed in the lush land of Burji. My dad and Mr. Dale had traveled to Burji in 2010. Trips to Burji generally made Alaba look easy. Mrs. Black's family had served in mission work in Burji, so her ties there were very strong. Oshe was a devout Christian who had become dear friends with the Blacks and other missionaries who had traveled to his homeland. A few years prior, Oshe had been given a choice. Muslims told him to stop speaking of Jesus. He refused and eventually a Muslim did run down his 8-year-old daughter in a truck. Oshe persevered and didn't renounce his Savior. He became even stronger through the tragedy of losing his daughter.

I looked into this man's eyes as he sat across from me on Marta's sofa, the warm outside breeze from the open windows blowing in the hum of outside insects. Oshe spoke softly. His eyes often brimmed with tears. The love of God was so evident and so overflowing from his soul that being in his presence made one feel closer to God. He reminded me of what one of the Apostles must have been like. He was like John the Beloved or even Paul. The visit with Oshe is one I will never forget.

The Church Protector and Old Tennis Shoes

The last Sunday we were in Ethiopia, the team joined my dad as he went to preach in a rural community called Bedene. The dusty, bumpy ride to the ninety-nine percent Muslim community proved to be a long one. When we arrived, I was surprised by how rural Bedene really was. I had been to many villages and this one could be classified as in "the middle of nowhere." We met the pastor of the church. Kadir was like Oshe. Though I didn't understand anything the man said, a faith and peace in God oozed from his attitude. The church in Bedene had been destroyed many times by the neighboring Muslims. Eventually, the church was afraid to rebuild because they knew it would be ruined again. Kadir stepped forward and said that if they rebuilt, it could be built on his personal land and he would protect it. He kept to his word. The Muslims threatened him, but Kadir never gave in. They came after him several times to beat him. One dark night, they beat him until they thought he was dead. Whether he was ever dead or God revived him, we don't know, but Kadir still lives. He never gave up protecting the church. My heart nearly broke as I watched him, dressed in his nicest clothes and holding his worn Bible as he hung on every word that came from my daddy's mouth. Kadir knew the true cost of commitment. He said these words to my dad after the service:

"I'm not afraid of man. My life is in God's hands. What can man do to me? Nothing. God controls my life."

I was overwhelmed by his testimony of faith. This same resilient faith was also evident in the compound we stayed.

We couldn't help but notice an elderly lady chopping wood outside of Marta and Demessie's house. The lady was bent over and clothed in torn, dirty clothes. The wood splintered apart as her weary back hacked at it. I felt guilty each time I walked by her. I wanted to take the ax from her hand and do it myself, but I knew that it was her job. She was given a place to live and food to eat for her work. What hurt the team's heart most was how her bare feet were callused and worn from the rough ground. This lady smiled when we walked by. She was so poor, but she was content.

The last night of our stay in Alaba, Marta prepared a large meal and many of the church's deacons and elders came and ate with us. The girls and women who had helped prepare the meal bustled around making sure everyone was eating. It was a loud and happy time. When the dishes had been put away, the Ethiopians pulled out gifts for us. Colorful scarves and skirts for the ladies and white tunics for the men. The givers of the gifts smiled, pleased with the way we doted over them. We gave gifts as well. They were small tokens of our love – things that we brought that would fit in an already bursting suitcase. Cindi pulled a pair of tennis shoes out and asked Marta to get the lady who worked outside chopping wood. Her face questioned us, but she went and brought in the lady. It was clear that she generally didn't come in the house during meal-time. She was shy as she waited for someone to explain why she was wanted. Cindi motioned for her to come near. Surrounded by the many people, she stepped forward as Cindi motioned to her feet and then back to the shoes she carried. The lady seemed shocked. Cindi insisted that they were for her and placed them in her hands. Tears rolled down her withered face. For the first time in a long time, maybe the first time ever, she was shown that she was special. I promised myself to never again look at old tennis shoes the same way.

Saying "goodbye" was never easy. We all shed tears when our suitcases were loaded and it was time to head back to Addis. Many of our friends gathered around as we prayed in a circle. We all said "amen" in unison. I had been sitting in the Land Cruiser, with my backpack smashed on my lap, when I felt something nipping at my heels. A snake! No, it wasn't a snake, because snakes don't "nip." I leaned way over and lifted a wool blanket up to see a chicken staring at me.

A chicken can't kill me, I don't guess.

Kandace laughed. I was proud of Kandace. She had come a long way. Through the entire two weeks I had watched her grow and mature. She finally saw what I had seen two years before. Her eyes were opened to the power of true Christianity in a foreign land. She was touched by the people and amazed by God's grace.

The orange ball of fire in the western sky sank below the African horizon, completing the last day of our trip. The following day, I put on my last clean outfit. It felt fresh on my clean skin as we headed for the Addis Ababa airport. As we were passing some time until we were supposed to board the plane, I noticed the elastic band in my skirt was becoming incredibly itchy on my skin. I was scratching my waist like a mad woman. I asked Daddy what he thought was going on. His facial expression changed.

"I didn't want to worry you, because I know how you are with bugs and such …."

I just stared. What? He continued:

"Well, there were bedbugs on my bed in Alaba. That was why I wouldn't let you and Kandace sit on my bed. That is why I asked for your large comforter. The thickness of it held them off for a while, but not for a long time. So, you probably have bedbugs …. I just assumed they wouldn't follow us to Addis."

He showed me the many bites on his back. They were exactly like mine. I started to panic. 20 hours on an airplane … with bedbugs? Dad told me to relax. I suddenly realized that my clothes were infested and I had nothing to wear. About that time, Daddy whispered in my ear that Cindi was sick in the bathroom. My mind was clouding with panic.

Dad, Kandace, Abigail and I went on a hunt to find me a new outfit. I found a silky, brown skirt with an authentic African flair. I was hoping to come across a shirt that was similar. I ended up with a huge, yellow, boxy workout T-shirt. I was a sight, but I was comfortable. At the time, I was embarrassed, but weeks later, I laughed at my circumstances.

We boarded the huge plane. I ended up sitting beside Daddy while every one else was a few rows back. I was looking out the window, listening to the airline's tacky music. Without having a chance to stop myself, tears began to pour down my cheeks. Daddy asked what was wrong.

"Daddy, it's not getting easier. For some reason, I can't stop thinking about Josh."

I cringed at his face full of concern. I expected him to say the same thing he had said over a month before. He didn't. "I'll be honest, Kate. He was not who I had in mind for you. But I realize that God's plans are greater than mine and if He wants you in a relationship with Josh, then I believe He will work it out. You need to keep being Katy. You need to keep living and keep seeking God. If Josh has feelings for you then he needs to make those known to me."

Looking into my father's blue eyes, I was overcome with thankfulness for the freedom to share openly with him. He wasn't harsh or hurtful. He trusted my heart, yet he made it clear that he wasn't letting me go.

We made it through the long flight and short layover in Amsterdam. A few hours later, we landed in Atlanta, GA. The plane sat on the tarmac for a long time. Dad shocked us all when he said, "We have fifty-eight minutes until the next plane leaves for Raleigh."

I quickly calculated that we had to go through immigration, customs and baggage claim. Any of those things could take an hour on its own. It seemed highly possible that we would miss our flight. Dad said that we would rent a car and drive, but the thought of riding in a car for hours instead of a short plane ride made me want to cry.

As we walked through the airport, each obstacle between our plane and us fell away. The lines were short and everything went smoothly. Even still, we had mere minutes to get to our gate. I looked at the team and said, "I am done walking. I am not letting us lose our plane because we refused to run."

I gripped my backpack and took off at full speed. Kandace and Abigail fell in behind me. We ran to the gate as a few of the last passengers were boarding. I held our spot as the remainder of the team meandered to the gate.

As we boarded, Dad's phone rang. I could tell he was talking to Mom. He got off the phone as we plopped down in our seats. I had heard Dad's side of the conversation and I was confused. I was turned away when Dad spoke, "Your Mom said that Josh has been moved to Meridian, Mississippi for 2 1/2 months. Mom said that he came through this airport just a few hours before us."

I was glad Dad couldn't see my face. I had been awake longer than I could think and I had been through an emotional and exhausting two days … two weeks. I just wanted to be home. I just had to keep it together a while longer.

Think of Oshe. Think of Kadir. You are blessed Katy Brown. Remember that.

We finally landed in Raleigh and walked toward the signs and smiling friends from Bethel Hill Baptist Church. Dr. Black laughed when he saw me.

"I like your outfit, Katy!" he bellowed.

Home

While we had been in Ethiopia, America had celebrated Thanksgiving. Many people had decorated for Christmas and the autumn breeze had turned into a winter chill. Mom welcomed us home as midnight approached. I will forever remember how my cleaned room smelled like cinnamon. Mom had placed a miniature Christmas tree in the window and had made my plush bed. I fell into the sweetness and closed my eyes. I forced my mind to forget all that burdened my heart. I was home. That was enough for now. One thing I knew, my feelings for Josh were stronger than the distance that came between us. My love for the country I had just left was stronger than the separation that now stood between us. I would cling to that truth and to the truth that God would take care of me. He would take care of us. All of us.

11

AN INTENTIONAL
RELATIONSHIP

Home Again

I woke up to see the ceiling of my room. Only two words entered my mind.

Home and Internet

My bedroom was warm and cozy as I opened my laptop. It felt odd to get on the computer. It had been refreshing to go without technology for a couple of weeks. The pressures of the world had washed away as I had been free to serve. No distractions, constant notifications or emails. Yet, here I was. The blinking cursor beckoned me to write to Josh. I typed him a short message, telling him that I hoped all was going well and that we had a great trip.

He responded. I was so happy when I saw his message come in. He told me that he had prayed for us while we were gone. I smiled to myself when I read how much he had enjoyed flying on a plane for the first time. While I had been in Ethiopia, he had been in Marine Combat Training, huddled in cold, dark forests with a rifle for a pillow. He had been sick during training. I wasted no time describing how Kandace had gotten sick too. We laughed at our circumstances and how much we had been through since we had last talked. Then we were more somber as he typed about missing home and the worldly, lost condition of the many marines around him. I could almost see him smile as he mentioned that a friend of his had accepted Jesus as his Savior in church. Ryan was his name and Josh had become a good friend to his new brother.

I tried to get back in the swing of school, but it was overwhelmingly difficult to concentrate. Josh and I messaged sporadically. He told me that his classes wouldn't really begin until January, so he spent a lot of time doing nothing. I asked him if he might get to come home for Christmas. He said he didn't know.

Church was decked out in Christmas decorations when we finally arrived for the first time since the trip. Mr. Dale, Dad, Kandace and I shared in the service. Tears trailed down my cheeks as I basked in the true miracles and wonder of the last couple weeks. The congregation laughed when they saw the tiny log bridges we crossed to go to villages and they pulled out tissues when we shared about Oshe, Kadir and the many others who had given all of themselves to serving Christ.

My friends, Jason and Katie Church, were talking to me after the service.

"I sure miss Josh." The words came out of my mouth before I had even thought about them.

Jason looked into my eyes with a decisive face. "I believe he will be home for Christmas, Katy."

His words surprised me.

He continued. "If there is any way for him to get home, I believe he will get here. He wants to see you too."

His words sunk into my heart and I tried to believe it.

As much as my mind wanted to linger on Josh, I knew better. I had to hold my heart together. I studied for upcoming tests and learned lines for the church Christmas play. Everything was going to be okay.

Josh kept telling me that he was going to do everything he could to come home for Christmas. Mama told me that it seemed like wishful thinking. It would be too much money to buy airfare. But, on this rare occasion, Mama was wrong. On December 9, 2011 he told me that he would be home in eight days. He would arrive home on the 17th and would be here 12 days. I knocked my chair over as I read the words and jumped around my bedroom like a little girl.

He made it clear that this visit would probably be the last one for at least six months. I was surprised by how easily I took that news.

Yeah, and at Halloween you told me that it would be a year until you would see me. Things are never as bad as they seem.

I comforted myself with those cheerful thoughts. Dad and Mama talked with me one day and encouraged me to be careful not to chase after him. Their advice led me to make a list of four things to do while Josh was home. In my journal, I scribbled this list:

1. Let him come to me.
2. Do not get overly attached.
3. Watch his attraction to me.
4. Watch his spiritual maturity.

That list proved to be some of the wisest words I could have written. I had observed other girls and the way they followed the boys like puppies. That wasn't going to be me. God was no fool; He knew every step of my life, including what Josh would become to me. I didn't push this.

December 18, 2011
Guess who I saw all day? Josh! He spent all day with my family. This morning I could hardly walk up the stairs to my Sunday School classroom where I knew he would be. I have never been more anticipant in my life ... even more so than when I saw him after boot camp. When I opened the door, there he sat. He smiled at me as though he had been waiting for me. I had to fight every urge to grab him up and hug him.

I never got a chance to talk to him all morning with a hundred things to do. Finally, I stood in front of him after the service. It was a little awkward. I told him that I was sorry for not getting to speak to him earlier. He came home with us for lunch. We warmed up to each other and we talked more. There was a vibe in the air. This feeling that if we had been alone, we would have talked forever. He may have come for lunch, but he stayed until 8:30 p.m. It began to feel so perfectly good and familiar. He was so good with Clara and Andrew. He fits right in.

I'm so excited and joyful. Christmas is all so bright! God answered my prayer and Josh is home! Even if the next week and a half only proves that we are friends, I'm still so happy!

The following night was Bible Study. I remembered vividly the last Bible Study we had been to together ... Halloween night. It had been a painful night, but one that seemed to change the course of the future. I asked Josh why he had come home. He shrugged and said, "I wanted to be home for Christmas." Yet, it was quite clear that he had very little to do while he was in town. Having come from a very fragmented family, there wasn't a nice cozy home to go to with a warm and loving family. The church was truly a second family to him. My house was becoming a second home.

'Tis the Season

"I just don't know," Dad's voice came over the phone.

"He doesn't have much to do! Please?"

"Remember, you are just friends."

"I will." I smiled.

So, Josh joined my family on a bowling outing in the few days before Christmas. We all got along so well together. In the past, Josh had always lingered by my dad's side. Now I was happy to see that Josh preferred my company even to my dad's company. He joked about my obsession with using hand sanitizer every time I touched one of the grimy bowling balls. He smiled when the ball rolled into the gutter nearly every time I sent it spiraling toward the pins. We all enjoyed his company.

On the Wednesday before Christmas, the church held a Christmas party for all of the children. After stuffing our faces with cupcakes and candy, we had a devotion and I helped as the little children fidgeted restlessly and their eyes hung onto the inflatable slide and bouncy house behind them. With the words, "you're dismissed," they took off at lightning speed.

I sat back and watched all of the excitement. I usually worked to keep the kids from killing one another on the oversized toys, but I just relaxed as younger teenagers took my role. Josh was talking with another couple a few tables away. They laughed and joked. I watched Josh. He smiled and nodded. It came to my mind yet again that he was different now than he had been years before. He was more serious and mature, a few added wrinkles on his handsome face. Yet, somewhere deep inside, he was the same ole Josh. I had looked away to think when I heard his voice beside me.

"Whatcha doing?" he asked.

"Just hanging out," I answered. I waited for him to nod and then walk off and find something more entertaining to do. But he stayed. Before either of us knew it, we had talked nearly the entire party. We leaned forward in interest as we shared. A few adults winked at me as they passed by.

They think we like each other. They think I am dating.

My chest lurched. I had spent so many years holding my heart and protecting my emotions. I didn't want others to think that I was letting them shatter on a whim. Remembering what I had written in my journal, I prayed that God would give me the strength to let Him lead.

That night, when all was cleaned up and we were home, Dad said plainly. "It's obvious you two like each other." I couldn't tell whether I should smile or frown.

Christmas Eve was one day away. Josh and I messaged each other about our plans for Christmas Eve.

"I guess I'll just hang out here," he said.

"Here" was his mom's house. I cringed. I knew that he didn't want to be there for Christmas Eve. They would do nothing but sit there and watch TV. He sounded sad and it hurt my heart. I wanted him to have somewhere to go and something to do. He would never ever ask for anything no matter how much he wanted it. It was more than my selfish desire to have him by my side. I loved Josh. I wanted him to enjoy Christmas. An idea came to my mind; one that my parents were likely to object to.

Mom nodded understandingly as I explained my idea.

"So can you ask Dad?" I pleaded.

She sighed. "I'll try. We all need to be in agreement on this, but I hate to think of Josh spending his Christmas alone."

Amazingly, Dad said "yes."

We were on our way to my grandparents' house on Christmas Eve, Josh in the van with us. I smiled to myself as I remembered the conversation Josh and I had only a couple days earlier. He had surprised me. When I had anticipated a quiet declination, he had given a cheerful, "I would love to go!" It was pleasing to know that he was happy with the arrangement.

But why is he so excited to join my family as we go to my grandparent's house?

It seemed odd. This 23-year-old was very chipper to be with us. Then again, Josh wasn't like the average, 23-year-old American male. He loved being around people of all ages. He loved "family" and that drew me to him.

The chilly wind whipped our coats as we pulled the shiny presents out of the trunk. MeMaw and PaPaw welcomed us along with the rich aroma of delicious food. A night of fellowship, smiles and full bellies followed. It wasn't at all awkward or stressful with Josh present. Once again, it felt as though he belonged. Everyone welcomed him. It felt like a dream come true as he joked with my family. The fact that he was happy was the best part of all. Wrapping paper and bows flew as everyone opened their gifts. While the little ones played with their new toys, PaPaw pulled his large bass out from the corner of the room. I took the hint and told Kandace to grab her violin while I went for my guitar. We had remembered to bring our instruments upon PaPaw's request. The out of tune strings found their correct pitches. We sang and played Christmas songs, old hymns and new praise songs. The evening ended and we packed our gifts up and hugged goodbye. Josh raved about what a good time he had. When he got out of the van, he waved and smiled. I could see the twinkling light of his mom's tree in the trailer. I smiled and pressed my palm against the cool glass of the window.

I want to decorate a tree with him one day. Just him and me.

As soon as the thought entered my mind, it flickered away. That night I hung my new red dress on my closet door. It looked beautiful and I knew that Josh would say that I looked beautiful. I practiced the song that I was going to play the following morning at church. It was always interesting when Christmas fell on Sunday, because as a pastor's family, we were always very busy. The jazzy piano piece was smooth and my voice sounded healthy and smooth. If it could only stay that way.

The following morning came. Christmas Day. I curled my long brown hair and slipped the form fitting dress over my head. Perfect. I spun around slowly in front of my mirror. "Pride comes before a fall," says the verse and so it did for me. A wide, greasy white line was on both hips.

Deodorant.

No!

I ran downstairs into my parent's bedroom. I paid no mind to how loud my voice was as I raged.

"Look what I've done! I ruined my dress!"

Mom calmly looked it over. We sponged and wiped, but it wasn't coming off. I was crying and my hair was damp with sweat. Mom had to move on to other things and I was left to deal with my mess alone. I soaked the stains and then blow-dried them. There were still two dark circles on either hip, but it didn't matter now as the time ticked. When I arrived at church, no one seemed to notice and several said that I looked pretty. I grinned when I saw Josh all dressed up in his uniform. It was vintage; the army green sweater so soft and sweet for a marine. His eyes looked me innocently over and he said sweetly, "You look very nice." I said the same to him.

I enjoyed every second of playing my song for the church. The notes felt smooth. The projectors cast a video of snow falling over the walls of the church. It was delicate and beautiful. Josh touched my shoulder from the seat behind me as I sat down from playing.

"Beautiful."

For a moment, I wondered if he meant the song or me. When the congregation stood to sing, my heart leapt as his slightly off-pitch voice met my ears. Tears rushed to my eyes as I whispered thanks to God for such a wonderful Christmas gift.

Bringing it to Light

Katie and Jason Church asked all of the Bible Study members if we
would like to go bowling just a few days after Christmas. Most of
the group was still busy with Christmas festivities, so it ended up
being four of us: Jason, Katie, Josh and me. Daddy wasn't so thrilled
about it seeming so much like a "double date." I didn't want to dis-
please Dad, because through the last few months I had committed
to make sure that he knew my feelings about Josh. We decided that
I would go, but I would be very careful how I acted with them. I
wouldn't be a foolish girl; I was a woman with purpose.

Josh probably thought that I was more reserved than usual,
but it didn't matter. It was more important that I kept my heart
intact until I knew for sure if he cared for me. I couldn't help but
laugh at our silly stories and poor bowling attempts. Every moment
I treasured, realizing that the moments I had with Josh would soon
be distant memories.

The following morning, I sat on my bed with my cell phone in
my lap. My fingers shook as I texted my dad. Daddy was just minutes away from picking Josh up for the men's Wednesday Lunch
Bible Study and I had to text him before Josh was there with him.
I knew it was time. I couldn't wait anymore. Daddy agreed with
me and said that he thought it was a wise decision. We needed to
know Josh's intentions. Dad would handle it. I waited all afternoon
for a text back. The day slipped by as I got ready to go to church
for the Wednesday night service. It would be the last time I would
see Josh during his visit. I curled my hair and smoothed out my
pretty pink sweater.

One look at his face and I knew. His smile was the brightest,
broadest one that I had seen on his face. He didn't say much; he
just looked at me differently. I wanted to ask what he had said to
Dad! I had waited so many months … years … and the answer
was waiting. It had to be a good sign that he was smiling so much.

The service was over and I was standing in front of the glistening Christmas tree. Josh was standing there beside of me. There
seemed to be a never-ending line to hug him and say goodbye – like

he was going to be gone forever. My heart hurt. When there was a moment of solitude, he turned to me and said, "Your Dad and I had an interesting conversation today."

I acted "dumb."

The ornaments and lights twinkled behind him. "It was good. It was something we needed to talk about."

"That's good. So, there isn't anything you could tell me about it?"

He laughed. "Ask him about it."

Then it was time for him to go. Or maybe he didn't have to leave just yet, but the tense, thick awkwardness couldn't be handled another moment. We looked at each other, wanting to say so many things and knowing that neither of us could utter a word. I could feel the hurt already. He hugged me quickly and turned to leave. I watched him as he walked toward the doors. He looked over his shoulder one last time and gave a wave.

"Come on, Katy. You're late for choir practice," someone said as they passed.

I stretched a fake smile across my face and went to the empty, upstairs restroom where I stood in a stall. My back pressed against the cold metal door, I let a few tears run down my face. I swiped them before they dripped on my sweater.

That night, after church, I stepped into Mom and Dad's room. They knew why I was there. Daddy was very unemotional about it all. He tried to give me his famous "bottom line," but even Mama told him that was ridiculous and insisted that he say more. Even though he was monotone, I could picture each moment of his conversation with Josh earlier that day with colorful imagination.

Dad had pulled into a parking space before the Bible Study and had said firmly, "Josh, we need to talk. How do you feel about Katy?"

Josh's heart rate skyrocketed as he glared ahead through the windshield.

My daddy spoke as he gathered his thoughts. "I sense that you and Katy like each other in a way that is more than just good Bible Study friends."

Josh swallowed the dryness in his throat as he answered, "I do like her. I am just not sure.... There are just so many reasons why I shouldn't. I am living so far away right now, I don't know what my future holds and she is also quite a bit younger than me ... but Kathryn is really mature. I do like her, but I guess that I've been trying to push those feelings away."

Dad nodded kindly as he looked at Josh, but Josh just stared straight ahead – right leg bouncing up and down. "Well, you probably realize that Katy likes you too. Until she marries, her heart is mine to protect and that is what I must do. So, I just want you to pray about this. Seek the Lord on what He wants for the relationship. Before you pursue Katy, I want to know your intentions. Don't worry, God will show you."

Daddy patted Josh on the shoulder and smiled.

The stress and weight began to roll off of Josh's shoulders. It had been so simple. Josh later said that my daddy had made it so comfortable and easy. Josh smiled and looked into my Dad's eyes, "Yes, I'll do that. I'll pray and He'll show me the way."

That night I scribbled in my journal:

December 29, 2011
.... Five years ago I would have sawed off my right arm to get to hear that. I just can't believe it. But, I have to keep my head on and know that it may not be God's will. I too need to pray and keep living .... Yes, with God's strength, I'll keep living. May absence make the heart grow fonder.

Growing Closer

When I saw Josh's name flash "online" on Facebook, I sent him a message. He had only been gone a day, but I wanted to make sure he had made it back to Mississippi, even though I knew he had from the pictures he had put online.

Talking online became a habit as 2011 slipped into 2012. We typed until our fingers ached. I spent a lot of my words on encouraging him to focus on Jesus. He admitted that he was struggling being the only Christian. Everyone else was full of dirty jokes and crude language. I prayed for him as he battled through the current of worldly Marines. I reminded him that he could be a light in the darkness, if he would only let God use him. I watched him grow closer to the Lord each day. I enjoyed being a helper and encourager.

One night in January, my chat box blinked of a new message, "Is it bad that I feel like I am going to have a heart attack every time I talk to you?" My eyes blinked in surprise.

Dad told me to be careful. "Don't give your heart away, Kate." Mom wrote a note and laid it on the kitchen bar.

Let him lead. If he cares for you, then he isn't going to let you go.

Though it nearly killed me, I backed off. I didn't talk to Josh as much. I wanted to see if he really wanted to talk to me as much as I did to him. For a few days he didn't talk to me much at all. Apparently he missed me because he soon became the initiator. It felt good to let him lead our conversations. He was thoughtful as he frequently said, "I just don't want to do anything wrong." I was thankful for his concern for my heart.

NYC

On January 11, 2012, Mama, Kandace and I flew to New York City. Kandace and I had been given the once in a lifetime opportunity to sing in Carnegie Hall. The Annie Moses Band had arranged for a choir and orchestra of a broad variety of musicians and singers to join them on one of the grandest stages in the world. Kandace and I, along with our dear friends Jessica, Natalie, Lydia and Valerie Hall would perform in a massive choir. The Hall Sisters, as they are called, formed their own incredible family quartet and was mentored by the Annie Moses Band. They blossomed into a professional group with gorgeously smooth harmonies. To us, they were wonderful friends.

NYC shimmered with winter beauty as we took our bus ride to the hotel, which was in the hub of the city and only a short walk from Times Square. It seemed too good to be true as we stepped into the sparkling lobby. Friends from the Fine Arts Summer Academy hugged us with glee. We were thrilled to see so many had been able to make the trip to New York.

We had only four days to see the sites and learn all of the music for the show. Rehearsals lasted through the mornings and early afternoons. The first day, we explored NYC. I had never seen so many people in my life. China had been abundantly populated when we had gone to get Clara and Andrew, but these small few miles of bright screens and lighted buildings, made everywhere else look so dark and empty. I couldn't imagine a place more energetic and bright.

The following day we went to see the Broadway show *Wicked*. My love for theatre and drama tingled through my body as I experienced one of the greatest dreams of my actress heart. The third day of our visit, we rode on the subway to go to the Empire State Building. What I expected to be my least favorite part of the trip quickly became the second best part, aside from singing on the Carnegie Hall stage. I had never been colder in my life as we stepped onto the top of the building. The sub-zero degree wind whipped at my skin; however, the coldness couldn't dampen the sights. The sun had set and the lights of the city stretched out as far as my eyes could see. I felt like I was above the world. My imagination burst with the images of soaring over the city, down the Hudson River, gliding like a bird on the cold air.

The next morning we spent time enjoying ourselves. It was only a few hours until our last rehearsal and then the performance. We, along with friends, went to Central Park. We skated on the ice until our parents reminded us that we better not get hurt before the concert.

When we stepped onto the stage for the first time, I felt that my eyes couldn't take it all in. The golden glow and red velvet of the most magnificent hall in the world took my breath away. After a run through all of the pieces and a taste of all we would experience in a few hours, we went to get ready for the concert. Kandace and I dressed in our long black gowns, curled our long hair, put on stage makeup and glamorous jewelry. I felt pure NYC. Mom and Mr. and Mrs. Hall told us goodbye as we entered the backstage doors. After showing our special passes, we were led to a large room bursting with singers and musicians. The wait seemed to go on forever. We filed out in perfect uniformed lines to our seats onstage. Then the music came. I couldn't imagine a place more designed for music. So many voices and instruments lifted the purest, most glorious sound to God. Tears of joy burned my eyes as we sang praises to His name before thousands. When it was time for our small ensemble to take the front of the stage for our cheery, fast paced *I'll Fly Away*, I soaked in how the moment felt. It felt like heaven.

In a split second, my mind flew back to Ethiopia. Kandace and I had been in Ethiopia only two months before. There we had stood in the most remote parts of the world listening to the raw, native voices of new Christians. That had been heaven as well. And now we stood in the magnificent Carnegie Hall. How could both be like heaven? It was simple. Where the Holy Spirit is present, so is the joy that comes with heaven. After the ring of the final note had faded away, we left the stage and joined everyone outside to wait on the buses to pick us up. Everyone spoke in loud, joyful voices as we congratulated and praised one another. The cruise boat was a medium size, perfect for a three-hour ride. The freezing air made us all the more anxious to step aboard. It was a dream as the boat slid softly along. The lights of NYC shimmered on the cold dark waters out through the long windows. Frank Sinatra and big band music filled the rooms and spread out onto the deck. We ate heartily and sat at the fancy tables. Kandace trotted off with her friends. I felt the exhaustion of the day pull on my eyelids as time inched past midnight. Dancing broke out on the dance floor and I hopped up to take part. We all laughed and danced until our sides hurt. Even Mama joined us. It was fun to dance to clean music with Christian friends.

As I sat back down and talked with Mr. and Mrs. Hall, a few people shouted beside me, "The Statue of Liberty! It's up ahead!"

I leaned forward. Sure enough, there she stood several hundred yards before us. I followed the crowd out to the deck as we watched the statue grow closer and larger. It was taller and more majestic than I imagined. *God Bless America* sounded over the speakers as we circled right under her. We all sang loudly with pride.

The cruise boat docked and we were all sad to say goodbye. The festivities were over. The bed looked like a cloud of fluff as I fell into its softness at 3:30 a.m.

We woke up a couple hours later and met the Halls to ride back to the airport. The short trip had felt longer than it had actually been. Each day had been packed with numerous adventures and experiences.

The Halls talked with me about Josh while we waited to board the plane. They knew that I had been talking with him. In fact, every spare moment of our time in NYC I had sat in the lobby of the hotel at one of the computers. There had not been access to Internet in the rooms, so while Kandace had hit the town with her friends, I had sat in the cold lobby messaging Josh online. We talked until Mom came and got me and forced me to go enjoy my time. Josh kept saying how much he hated to waste my time, but I told him that I wanted to tell him everything. It mattered so much to me that he was a part of my life. It had proven to be very difficult to maintain a healthy relationship with my family and friends while keeping him updated on most everything in my life. It was something I would learn to balance.

Jessica asked me to fill her in on everything. I tried to be realistic as I told her how I hoped that Josh and I would grow closer. She promised to pray for me.

I prayed constantly myself. I couldn't do much for Josh except pray. Sometimes it felt so futile and I cried that I couldn't do more. Once I was back home, I sent him a letter. I was careful not to sound too romantic. After all, Josh still hadn't told my daddy what his "intentions were." We were still considered friends.

We messaged until I couldn't take it anymore. In the latter part of January, we began to video chat. It was a blessing to be able to see him. His abode in Mississippi was cruder than I imagined. He had an annoying roommate who enjoyed walking past Josh and the laptop constantly. Whenever he pleased, he turned and stuck his face in the camera. Sometimes he would use bad language and

Josh would mute the video. I frequently saw Josh lean over and ask, "Could you stop that while I talk to her?"

One day, Josh broke the news that I didn't want to hear. He had been told where his potential permanent duty station would be. The possibilities were all over the place.

"So, it could be Japan, Hawaii, Arizona, California, possibly Virginia and maybe North Carolina."

I felt hope as the list went on. "North Carolina? Really? Please don't end up in Japan!"

Panic rose in my chest, elevating my heart rate as I imagined being away from Josh for three and a half years. Could we maintain a relationship thousands of miles apart without ever seeing each other? For a moment, I felt like I was already getting in way over my head.

He bashed my hope even further, "Well, I may not even get to choose. My instructors may choose for me. Either way, it will be determined in three weeks."

Since my parents had taught me by example that tough circumstances didn't mean give up. I wasn't satisfied. Every day of my life they had shown me how to push forward. I asked Josh, "Well, what can you do?"

"I must be at the top of my class. The higher I am, the more freedom I get to choose."

"Then do it," I said firmly.

Committed Hearts

Over the course of January I watched Josh become my best friend. I also watched myself teeter on the edge of a swirling, downward vortex of anxiety. I found myself sleeping poorly, eating less and struggling to focus on my last few months of high school. It was time for Josh to say something; it was time to make things official with me.

I was walking down the hall, headed towards the basement to go get something, when Dad's voice floated up the stairwell.

He's practicing his sermon.

"I am glad to know your feelings …"

Josh. He is talking to Josh.

I battled whether I should stay and listen.

"You have my consent to pursue a relationship .... I think you should tell her how you feel."

Goosebumps spread over my skin. I heard the phone beep as they hung up.

It's just a matter of time before he asks me to be his girl! He talked to Daddy!

January 29, 2012

In shock. It finally happened. After countless journals, tears and six years Joshua Clint Isaacs told me that he cares deeply for me. We were talking on Skype and he told me that we needed to have a serious conversation. My legs have never shaken so much. My whole body shook when he said, "I have feelings for you." My heart almost burst.

I told him everything. Maybe I shouldn't have, but there was no stopping. I even told him how I shredded my journals about him. He said that he knew when I was 12 that I liked him. He started feeling an attraction to me a year and a half ago! That is way longer than I imagined. He told me that he hated Parris Island, but he would go back there today just for the letters I sent him. He said he came home to see me in December. His whole class knows he cares for me, because he talks about me so much. He said that he is committed to me.

I told him in detail about the last six years. I felt led to tell him that I am "whole" and I know that he isn't completely whole. I told him how a year ago I wouldn't have dreamed of liking someone who isn't like me ... perfectly whole. But, the Lord has changed my heart. Even though I wouldn't trade anything for my unscarred heart, if the man I marry has a scarred heart, it's okay. I told him that he is healed and I'm good with a healed heart.

And guess what? He started crying. I wanted to reach through the screen and wipe away his tears. But, they were good for him. There was a presence of peace.

I'm still in shock. The man he is, though battered and bruised, is the man I've loved. Knowing that we feel the same way about each other after all this time makes me feel like I'm flying. I just want God's will done. It matters most.

We were officially committed to each other with the pursuit of a relationship clearly underway. The end of January was full of exams for Josh. I waited with baited breath as I anticipated his test results. His future hinged on it. He made a 94, 98, 100, 96 and 98, respectively. He surged to the top of his class. We talked often. He said sweeter things to me, but as much as I wanted to hear romantic words, he was careful to limit them. I nearly cried when he told me that he never again wanted me to feel like I had to follow him around as I did when I was 11 and 12.

His voice wavered as he said, "I want you to be by my side."

After all, life is a journey. It's a long walk. Walking by him would be my honor.

Life was a fog in early February. I was overwhelmed with school, responsibilities and the fact that Josh might soon be assigned to a far off duty station. I was given the part of Mary Magdalene for the church *Passion Play*. The extravagant, huge play was held every year around Easter and depicted Jesus' life, death and resurrection. Many came to Christ yearly. This particular year I would have more lines than anyone. The story would be through Mary Magdalene's eyes. I enjoyed every moment of planning, acting, singing and performing. It helped divert my mind from my other pressures and worries.

On February 6, 2012, Josh sent me a message saying he had his orders. His home for the next three and a half years had been decided.

"Where?" I begged. I waited, feeling my pulse pound my brain.

"Cherry Point, North Carolina."

I laid my face on the keyboard and wept tears of pure joy. For the first time in my life, I was confident that I would marry Josh Isaacs.

Over half of his class had been sent to Japan. He had chosen North Carolina for one reason … me.

I began to miss Josh as time went along. Since we had begun a serious, intentional relationship, my desire to look into his eyes and be near him was overwhelming. We grew in our relationship. Though it was painful at the time, I later became thankful that Josh and I had been forced to talk so much. The distance had made the physical aspect easy. There was no opportunity to compromise our boundaries.

I read a quote that I wrote in my journal: *Distance does to love what wind does to fire, it extinguishes the weak and feeds the strong* (Bob Marley).

One day in early March, Josh made me upset when he kept texting someone while we were talking. I curtly snapped that I wouldn't talk to him if he couldn't give me his attention. He said he was sorry and he wanted to talk to me. I broke into a million pieces. The stress and frustration of missing him exploded as I cried to the cold computer screen before me. Josh picked up his laptop. He laid the top of the screen against his chest. The camera was pressed against his shoulder. When I asked him what he was doing, he said softly, "I'm hugging you as you cry."

Time passed. Josh told me that he hoped to come home in April or May. Patience was getting harder to come by.

I wasn't the only one in my family in need of patience. Andrew had a surgery on his feet in early March. The muscles in his feet were reconstructed as his bones had been in the past. His feet were straightened and repaired from their clubbed state. He was placed in casts that went up to his upper thighs. My brother, who thrived off of running and playing, was forced for the second time in his life, to sit in a wheelchair as his legs healed for six weeks.

The morning of March 8, 2012, Josh told me that he had safely arrived at Cherry Point. The days in Meridian, Mississippi were finally over. He was so nervous as he signed in. He asked me to pray that he wouldn't make a fool of himself. He didn't.

Being only 300 miles apart seemed to make us more ready for things to move forward. We talked about marriage for the first time. We both had known and agreed that marriage was the end goal all along, but talking about it made it seem so real and close.

"I'm not sure I can wait three years. That's an awfully long time," he said.

I agreed. I didn't need to be reminded that I was only a few weeks from turning 18 years old.

Daddy sat on his bed that same night. Mom and Andrew were still at the hospital from the surgery. Dad had been sick with the flu and was finally well enough to be coherent.

"Do you love him, Kate?" Dad asked.

I thought before I answered. Daddy's eyes probed me, but I could tell that he cared greatly how I felt. This moment would never be forgotten.

"I do, Daddy."

"Does he love you?"

"Yes, I believe so. He hasn't said so yet. He is waiting till he sees me in person."

"Could you have his children? Move away from all you love and know to be with him?"

The moment of truth. Could I give it all up? This was more than a mushy, romantic dating relationship. This was marriage. Why be in a relationship just for recreation, anyway? Only broken hearts come from that. The question still stood. Could I leave it all for Josh Isaacs? I felt the Holy Spirit loosen the words in my throat.

"Yes, I could."

Daddy nodded, tears twinkling in his blue eyes.

The thought of leaving my family already burned my chest with pain. Only God would have the power to give me the strength to overcome it.

12 PROMISING FOREVER

"I love you"

March seemed to be never ending. The days leading up to the church's annual Passion Play were stressful. One minute Josh was coming home for Easter and the next he wasn't coming home at all. One night as we talked, he poured out his heart. All of his friends were partying. He vented on how they did the least amount of work possible while he worked all of the time. I encouraged him to pull through. We were so close to Easter. Though I wondered if he would really make it home, I prayed with all of my heart that he would.

The *Passion Play* weekends came. We preformed two weekends, on Saturday and Sunday nights. I was so nervous as I stood backstage. Hundreds of words jumbled up my brain, yet somehow they all smoothed out and came clearly as I spoke. I enjoyed every moment. I reminded myself that Josh would be home soon.

The day I had awaited all winter finally came. Josh was coming home for Easter. On April 6, 2012, Daddy and I drove an hour to Winston-Salem to pick him up. A friend was dropping him off on his way home. I had imagined a thousand times how we would run to each other and fall into each other's arms.

The car pulled up and I stepped closer, anticipating. It seemed too good to be true. We didn't run to each other. I did a silly gallop and he glided around the car. He embarrassingly said, "Well, hey!"

He pulled me to him and embraced me, whispering in my ear, "I've missed you."

Daddy, Josh and myself all got in the car. I remembered when Dad and I used to pick Josh up before church. I had always sat in the passenger seat and Josh had sat alone in the back. Today I would sit with Josh. We had never been together with the understanding that we were interested in marriage. It was incredible looking over at him and thinking:

He could be my husband.

We left the middle seat between us empty. It signified something to us – each step in our relationship is worth great consideration and thought. Some things are worth taking time. That first day we just talked and smiled. His eyes drifted over my face. Our relationship was all so fresh and new.

He stayed at our house until late that evening talking with the family and me. I didn't want to see him go, but I knew I would see him again in a few hours. Daddy and I took him to his mom's trailer and I prayed that he would find somewhere relatively comfortable to sleep.

The next day was a warm, sunny Saturday. We picked him up and went to the church Easter egg hunt. It was then that we decided to let people see us together. We didn't touch each other ... didn't even hold hands. Just knowing that he wanted to hold my hand was enough for now. People teased as we stood side by side. It was funny to me that we still talked so much. After three months of doing nothing but talking online, we talked more in person. My family loaded up the van and we went to get ice cream. Every moment with Josh was a precious gift. I knew our time was fleeting.

Easter morning I awoke with a smile in my heart. I dressed in my "graduation dress," which I had bought a few weeks earlier with my cousin Taylor. Josh dressed in his "dress blues." He looked stunningly handsome. Everyone at church was so excited to see him. I even sat beside him during the service. Mom snapped our picture in front of the church. I was so grateful for that picture months later. It was a treasure on the days when I wondered if we had even been together – if all of those hours had only been a good dream.

While my family relaxed that afternoon, I asked Josh if he wanted to go for a walk outside. We had never been "alone" before, even for a moment. Dad and I had already established what would be appropriate. Walking around the house and to the creek were acceptable, especially since my siblings were playing out there. We walked down the hill. My house could still be seen above us, as our eyes caught glimpse of the shimmering, cold water below. We talked about how much we had missed one another. After a few skipped stones, and the retrieving of a sterling silver ring that fell off of my finger, we headed back up the hill. Josh bumped my hand with his. I apologized, but he asked softly, "May I hold your hand?"

So there it was … our first time holding hands. His warm, strong hand was all I had ever dreamed. It reminded me of the conversation we had had months ago. He had told me that he just wanted to walk by my side. Here it was coming true. We walked past my grandparent's house. They lived next door to my family's house. I could feel them staring out the windows. Why wouldn't they? Could I blame them! There was nothing to be embarrassed about.

I felt tears of bewilderment constrict my throat. My dreams! We were walking down the gravel road I had always imagined walking with him. The spring sun dipped lower in the sky and the dogwood trees swayed in brilliant purity and whiteness. This had been my deepest heart's desire. I had prayed for this moment a thousand times years ago. I had imagined Josh looking into my eyes and whispering for the very first time, "I love you." God had stripped all those dreams away those years gone by. He had firmly required me to lay them down. My obsession with "love" had been destroying my love for the greatest Lover. He had known all along that my wish would come true. It would be greater than I ever dreamed, if I only did it His way.

The tall trees rose above us as we turned a corner to walk back up my driveway. Right on cue as if God had breathed it into his heart at the perfect moment, Josh turned slightly as he walked.

"I want you to know, Kathryn ... that I love you so very much."

So perfect. So pleasing and pure. So full of truth. I squeezed his hand. "I love you too."

The day after Easter was our last day together. Josh and I wanted to spend time together, but we had to figure out a creative way to do so. Kandace agreed to come with us to go to lunch. I refused to "date." I wasn't about to say that Josh and I were more mentally strong and emotionally stable enough to be able to go out alone for long periods of time. Especially in our early days together, Dad helped me talk Kandace into being our tag-along. Three is a crowd, but sometimes a "crowd" is a good thing.

We ate at a Mexican restaurant and then went for another walk in town. I felt like I had lost total control over my tear ducts. I couldn't stop crying. Kandace sat several feet off while Josh and I walked toward a bridge. He handed me a little blue bag. Inside was his marine graduation ring.

"I don't have much to give you to remember me by, but I do have this."

"It's perfect. I'll hold it when I miss you," I said.

"Could you take care of it for me till I can give you something better?"

It came time to take Josh back to Winston-Salem. Waiting on his friend's car was misery. In a fleeting moment, he was gone again. Just a few short days and it was over. A few hot tears ran down my cheeks on our drive home. I was so thankful to remember that Mom and Dad had planned a trip to the coast in a couple weeks after we had visited some friends in Raleigh and Virginia. I was going to get to spend time with him again.

Just a couple weeks.

Sometimes I put his ring on my finger while in my room. I talked to Josh everyday. I studied hard, trying desperately to accomplish all I could before May. It seemed nearly impossible to concentrate at times – another reason relationships should be chosen at a proper time, because they can drain one's brain of everything else important.

Daddy took me to lunch in mid-April. I assumed it was for my 18th birthday. It was, but he had other topics in mind. He forced me to think about the facts … like only a father can. Over our steamy Japanese food, he told me that he believed Josh will be deployed in the summer.

"Do you want to marry him before he goes?"

I swallowed hard. Questions swirled in my head like a tornado.

If he has to be deployed then we either have to get married in a couple months or potentially, a couple years.

The thought was frightening. How could I have a big wedding? Josh hadn't even asked me yet. I hadn't actually seen him in person but three days in our whole relationship! It was much to think about.

After my birthday, we took that promised trip to the coast. I wrote about it in my journal.

April 30, 2012

Where do I begin? There are too many wonderful things to say. Josh and I took advantage of every moment together. He took my hand immediately and never really let go unless we had to eat. The first night was short, but lovely. He gave me a small box with a beautiful light rose-colored watch in it. It is gorgeous.

We went for a walk around the hotel and on a path in the woods. You wouldn't expect anything out there, but as we walked we came upon a canopy of trees and a sparkling swamp of green water. It was beautiful. So different from the mountains of home.

He told me he can't believe that I love him and that I am so amazing. I laid my head on his shoulder. We walked down another path, passing people on the way. This one led to a peninsula surrounded by water and honeysuckles. We stood there a moment. Josh pulled his phone out of his pocket. Suddenly, one of our favorite songs was playing. The soft piano and guitar filled the air as he opened his arms to me. I put my hand on his shoulder and he put his on my waist. His eyes glistened. We danced. Surrounded by nature, we danced with tears in our eyes.

He twirled me and pulled me back and sang the words in my ear. The sweet, words so pleasing to the Father.

He also told me that he didn't know if I would make it to my 19th birthday without being married. When our time together was ending, it was so hard to stay strong … and cheerful. He typed on his phone a message so he wouldn't have to talk out loud. It said that the Lord is our strength. He tapped my chin and whispered, "Smile." I did.

Once at the barracks on base, he asked me to run to his room with him. I stood at the door while he grabbed a card. He told me to open it in the van. I hugged him tightly. Bitter pain choked me as I turned to go. I got in the van and he waved as we pulled away. Every part of me screaming to turn back, I opened the card. After the sweetest words I think I had ever read were the words "don't cry" and "don't worry." I buried my face in my hands and sobbed. Heaving, ugly tears. My family patiently waited.

I watched flat land turn to mountains. Home. But for the first time in my life, I felt that home was somewhere else.

I know it will be another month till I see him. I trust God. Josh does as well. Love is strong and God is stronger.

Wouldn't trade anything for that dance Saturday. I pray I'll never forget it.

Flowers and Diplomas

On May 3rd, my cousin Taylor and I graduated from high school. A large vase of flowers sat on the counter that morning. A little card was attached.

> *I'm so proud of you, sweetheart! I love you so much!*
> *Josh*

A part of me wanted to hug and kiss the flowers as though they were a part of him. We placed the flowers on my table at the graduation.

For years, since I had been little, many of my friends had told me that I would not end up "normal" if I was home-schooled. I used to cry that I had no "friends," because many considered me "weird." My mama kept homeschooling me anyway. She taught me with all of her strength. My schooling was unique in the fact that if I didn't understand something, I wasn't given a bad grade and forced to move on; I was sat down and was required to work on it until I understood. My schooling wasn't a cookie-cutter formula to fit dozens of children; it was designed for me. I wasn't a genius by any stretch of the imagination, but I wasn't dumb either. I thrived off of the natural, healthy way to learn. It wasn't a new revolutionary form of learning. Homeschooling is as ancient as the hills and was the only education known to man for centuries.

I felt pride and joy as I finally stood before many and proclaimed, "It worked! I made it to the end and it didn't kill me!"

Sharing His Load

Over the course of May, Josh and I grew a lot. Our relationship struck deeper ground. I learned a lot about his past. Many things he said made me cringe. He had been through so much in his childhood. His life had been almost totally opposite of what mine had been. While I had enjoyed years of a reliable, constant, close family, Josh had endured the struggles of an unreliable, inconsistent and broken family. As a child, he had quickly learned to rely only on himself. His mom and dad had not been married when he was born. They were products of the fast, rebellious lifestyle in the late 1970s and early 1980s. He was raised on roaring 80s music, the thick odor of second-hand smoke and the results of alcohol use. His parents loved him, but their focus wasn't on their son. Josh had been a cute boy with a blond bowl-cut. Most of his teachers remembered him for his acute ADHD (Attention Deficit Hyperactivity Disorder).

There were blessings connected with his inability to remain in one place too long. He developed an uncanny ability to avoid trouble. Countless nights passed with him lying on his worn bed, bags packed and ready for his father to pick him up. He hoped his dad would keep his promise every time, but the most of the time, the mornings came and his dad never showed up.

People came and went in his childhood. His mom's boyfriends pillaged and took. Sometimes they scared Josh so much that he was afraid for his mom's life. He often teetered near the edge of death. Many times, his mom was drunk and with her intoxication came anger. Josh frequently kept her from harm while putting himself in danger. Tears weren't enough. Being good wasn't enough. Nothing could change his circumstances, but in the middle of his messy childhood, he decided he would live a dramatically different lifestyle than his parents. He would grow up and leave it all behind. He wanted something different for himself.

Unfortunately, the baggage wasn't always so easy to drop. Josh found this to be true as he fought through years of fear of abandonment. Over and over again, I told him that I wasn't leaving. I was going to always be here. Little by little, he began to believe me enough to place trust in me. I was satisfied with a slow start. I had no baggage. There wasn't a better person to help him carry some of his.

The Waterfall

At the end of May, Josh came to visit again. Our family met him in Winston-Salem again since we were already there at a home-school conference. We enjoyed several days together. Things were changing. Marriage was an easy topic. On another walk to the creek in the late spring warmness, Josh asked how long it takes to plan a wedding.

"Well, many women prefer about five to six months to plan."

I knew that I didn't need that long, but I wanted him to realize that it wasn't a little party that could be thrown together with a couple hundred bucks.

"Really?" His eyes widened. "This kind of changes things. I didn't know it takes that long."

I rolled my eyes and laughed. I didn't want a wedding that would be thrown together. It needed planning and time.

While eating with his dad and sisters at a restaurant in town a few days later, his dad finally asked the question I had wondered for months.

"So Son, when's the big day?"

Josh didn't bat an eye. "Probably before the end of the year ... if Kathryn's okay with that."

This year?

I stared at him. I had imagined next spring or summer. I hadn't even considered before the New Year.

Once Josh had left again and I had spent two solid days missing him horribly, I felt much more content with getting married sooner. One day, I lost it. In my family's living room, I let my heart leak out all over everything. I begged forgiveness for the pain I had caused my family by letting the stress in my own life overtake me. I hadn't been myself. This wasn't how love was supposed to be. My love for Josh couldn't destroy my relationship with the people in my life who had loved me longer than anyone. They didn't know what I dealt with or the hurt I endured each time the man I loved left me, but that wasn't their fault. I told them everything and reminded them how much I needed and loved them.

June came along with the annual mission trip to Texas and Mexico. I was anxious to do something important. Jason and Katie had moved to Weslaco as missionaries and were living in the church's mission house. They had everything clean and shiny when we arrived. We enjoyed a wonderful trip. Josh and I talked as much as we could. With very limited cell reception in the houses, I sat outside in the over one hundred degree heat to talk to him.

I received a text as we came back across the border from Mexico one night.

"I am so excited. I just did something so amazing."

He bought my engagement ring.

Somehow I knew it without a doubt, but I didn't want to spoil everything for him, so I didn't say what I knew to be true.

At the end of June, Josh had to come home on an emergency trip to see his father and grandfather who been in a car accident. They were both in critical condition, but managed to survive and leave the hospital with months of recovery ahead of them. Josh and I spent a little over a day together while he was home. I was able to cope better when he left because I knew he would be home in a few days for the July 4th holiday.

He was so set on going to a waterfall when he got home on that hot Friday afternoon.

"I really want to go to a beautiful waterfall tomorrow morning," he said as he viewed waterfalls online.

I just smiled.

The next morning he acted jittery and nervous. Mom winked at me as he told me to bring some extra clothes in case it started to rain. He had his massive marine backpack slung over his shoulder. This man who always claims he doesn't need any extra clothes or anything was lugging this backpack around.

Suspicious.

We took off for the beautiful Cascade Falls on the Blue Ridge Parkway that afternoon. It was a special place dear to my heart. As a little girl, my family used to go there frequently. We had eaten many a picnic there. I had run down the rock steps many times with my sister and cousins.

It was different that day. The sky was cloudy. The sky drizzled a drop of rain occasionally.

As we sauntered down the narrow mountain path, he asked me when we could set the wedding date.

I chuckled and said, "Whenever you get around to asking me."

He laughed and said, "Oh, I will one of these days."

So, I bit my lip and pulled the spider webs out of my damp hair. We crossed a little bridge, the bridge I used to skip across. We came to the waterfall and Josh jumped over a couple bushes and shrubs to get a better picture straight down the falls. I yelled for him to be careful. He smiled. We stood there at the top of the falls, the mountains surrounding us.

Josh asked, "Is this the best view?"

"Um, the falls are a little prettier further down."

"Okay, can we go down there?"

We walked down the familiar rock steps. Josh told me to go first. He let me get a few feet ahead of him as he hung back. I gasped when I saw the gorgeous fall.

I had forgotten how beautiful the place was. Tons of clear, bluish water cascaded in magnificent glory over the rocks and down the steep mountain. The rich green of summer stretched down below us like a carpet.

Josh muttered how amazing it was.

I leaned against the rock wall. I let the wind blow by my face. I felt strange though. Josh was acting nervous. He stood behind me and we were silent. Just the sound of rushing water filled the air. Josh pulled me into a loose hug.

"Kathryn, my heart is beating so hard."

I was so gullible. "Well, we didn't walk that fast!"

He sighed and I leaned back to look into his face. His shoulders shook under my hands and his firm jaw was clenched.

He whispered, "I think I could dance to the sound of that waterfall."

I smiled and backed up to turn away and as I did his hand fell from behind my back. In his hand was small black box. My mind was slow to process, but I knew as soon as I saw his eyes fill with tears. The world moved in slow motion as he dropped to one knee. I clamped my hand over my mouth.

He opened the box to reveal a sparkling diamond ring, but that is not what I saw. I saw his face filled with love.

The moment came.

"Kathryn Brown, will you marry me?"

I said without hesitation, "Yes! Oh, yes!"

I tried to pull him up, but he stayed on his knees as he slid the ring on my finger.

While most couples kiss a passionate kiss after the question is popped, Josh and I hugged and said nearly in unison, "Saving that kiss."

He chuckled as he said that the ring box was too big for his pocket so he had to bring the backpack and had used bringing clothes as an excuse.

I was giddy walking back up the trail. I didn't cry. Like a little girl, I danced and skipped.

"Now can we talk about a date for the wedding?" Josh asked.

We had about established December as "the" month when we got home. My family hugged and congratulated us. Mama wasn't too happy about December. It was too soon. Josh and I talked about how much we didn't want to be apart. Daddy encouraged us not to wait too long. We began pushing the date up earlier. It landed on November 10th. Mom about got choked up, something that rarely happens to her.

Making everyone happy was nearly impossible. My family wanted me there and Josh wanted me with him. Why couldn't we all just be together? It wasn't that simple. I was going to be a Marine wife.

Eventually, November 10th sunk in. We had four months. Josh left again and it was the hardest goodbye by far. He gripped my hand until we had to let go. For a moment, I wanted to move the wedding even closer. I stared into my beautiful, half-karat, solitaire engagement ring. It's clarity was nearly perfect. Josh had chosen between clarity and size. He had told me that its purity mattered more than how big it was. I agreed. When the light hit the brilliant ring, it shot out with splendor.

On my bed lay a blue wedding planner and a few glossy wedding books Mama had bought for me. Flipping through them made one thing very clear: this was going to be a lot of work. Mama was like a lightning bolt. I had never seen anyone so driven to get things done. I wanted days and weeks to decide things. Being indecisive wasn't an option.

It was always a little awkward when people asked how old I was.

"18."

Their surprise wasn't well hidden. "Really? How ... nice."

I didn't care. I had always dreamed that I would get married at 19 years old. It was the perfect age. Some looked down their noses in jealousy and others whispered that I would crumble once I was out "on my own."

"What about college?"

That was the real question. I had already had several credits, but at this point I felt one goal. Get married. College had become an obsessive "must do." I wasn't convinced. Not everyone had to go to college at 18 or 19. More and more professionals were saying that college degrees were great and all, but not as necessary as people think. I planned to study after we got married, but I wasn't so worried about it. A few babies and a house of my own – that was good for me. The middle age career women in my life gasped and suggested I really think about the consequences.

Consequences. Okay.

I really would live without a college degree. Traditional and old-fashioned I may have been, but I was content.

We met with the photographer. I just about passed out on the cold café floor when she named her price. Mama said we would go with her. On the way home from the meeting, I asked her why she wanted to use such an expensive photographer.

"We can scrimp on a lot of things, but pictures are forever. Pictures will be what we will remember your wedding by for years after the food is gone, dress is yellowed and we're old. They need to be good."

Mama was right.

My family took off to Nashville, Tennessee about a week after Josh went back to Cherry Point. The Fine Arts Summer Academy was fantastic as it had been every year. Everyone congratulated me and asked about Josh. I was so proud to talk about my Marine fiancé, but it hurt just as deeply. I missed him. There were a few other engaged couples there and they were always together. I talked to Josh as much as time would allow and that wasn't enough.

I spent every spare moment looking at wedding dresses online. I wanted one white as white could be and modest. I wasn't interested in the halter look. If I wouldn't wear a halter to the beach, I wasn't going to wear one down the aisle. While sitting in rehearsal, I found a beautiful Cinderella princess dress on a wedding dress website. It was soft and sparkled with a magical shimmer. Several of the girls sitting around me agreed that it was beautiful. Mama liked it too.

Then she clicked on the one beside it. It was whiter, wasn't as full and was slightly more simple. The light fabric was gathered at the waist. The square neckline and flower petal sleeves were delicate.

Mama suggested that I go to a few stores and try on dresses, but for some reason, I had no desire to do so. Within a day I was confident which dress I wanted: the second one. I decided that the first was beautiful, but too much fluff and glitz. The second was perfect. The dress was worth over a thousand dollars, but we got an amazing deal on a floor sample. The sample was in perfect condition. Mom sent me a text in the afternoon during choir rehearsal.

"It's ordered."

Nearly everyone said I was crazy to order a dress that I had never seen in person and had never tried on. I agreed that it could have been a disaster. It was unlike me to be so risky, but there was no dress like it. I anticipated several weeks before the dress would arrive, but a couple weeks later and the box from Utah was on the doorstep. Panic surged through my chest as we opened the box.

White. It was so white. So beautiful. The chest and shoulders looked like running water that cascaded into a light, flowing chapel train. It had to fit. Mama helped me get into it. The long corset back took ages to tighten and tie. I turned toward the mirror. Tears in my eyes.

Absolutely perfect. I couldn't have been happier. God spoke into my mind.

Just like Josh will be your only kiss. Just as you have never tried on another man's love. You have chosen one dress and trusted that it would be perfect. One dress. One man. Thank you for trusting Me.

Mama's usual stoic face melted into a grin. "It looks great!"

Counting Down the Days

Josh called me on July 31, 2012. He was irritated about something, but wouldn't say what he was upset about. Finally, it came forth like a tidal wave.

"I have to go to Alaska."

He will miss our wedding!

"What?! When?"

"September. I'll be home at the end of October … a few weeks before the wedding."

Any chance of him coming home before our wedding flittered to the wind. Not only was he missing all of the decisions and work we were doing, but he would miss the remainder as well. One thing was good. The small deployment would likely help keep him from having to go anywhere immediately after we got married.

My mama and I worked together planning the wedding. I enjoyed making out lists of things I wanted for our house. We would be living in base housing. I wouldn't get to see our home until after our honeymoon. Josh planned our honeymoon. Since I had been a little girl, I had always joked that I wouldn't go stay in a cabin in Gatlinburg, Tennessee like my parent's had done. When Josh asked if a cabin in Gatlinburg, Tennessee sounded good. I laughed. It sounded wonderful. He sent me pictures of the cozy cabin and my excitement grew.

In mid August, more deployment news came. Josh would more than likely have to go on a seven month long deployment to Afghanistan in June of 2013. It was over nine months away, but it still didn't stop the sobs in my chest. We would only get half of our first year together. A thought captured my mind.

What if we have a baby while he is gone? I would be alone! God, you wouldn't allow that would You?

I realized that people do it all the time, but it didn't make it any easier in my mind. Yet, Josh encouraged me not to worry. But the Evil One whispered that was like telling a fish not to swim.

It was a long drive to the beach in August. Mama and Daddy had saved up to go on a trip and they had chosen Atlantic Beach since it was only 30 minutes away from Cherry Point. It provided a perfect opportunity to get in some of the pre-marriage counseling sessions, which Dad required before the wedding. Every afternoon, as soon as Josh was off work, Dad and I drove to get him. He spent each evening with us at the condo on the beach and right before bedtime, we drove him back to his barracks. We enjoyed our time together celebrating his 24th birthday, which had passed a few days before. I gave him a small charm to go on his dog tags. The smooth sliver had words etched into it.

"I love you. Forever yours, Kathryn."

The weekend came and he spent it with us on the beach. Sometimes Josh and I walked down the beach and on the pier together with my family behind us. When no one was there and we were barely out of sight, we found how easy it was to hold each other closely. It would be so easy to break our promise. It would be so easy to kiss. Just when I thought I could, when the power and desire seemed to be swelling like the tide, we broke apart and said firmly to one another, "Let's go."

Never had I been more convinced that dating in its typical American form is dangerous. Being alone leaves a lot of room for faltering. Even the strongest are rarely strong enough to overcome the hardest of tempting circumstances. I was thankful that we chose to stay close to family once we had seen the temptations.

It was time to say goodbye again. Everyone hugged Josh outside of the barracks. I didn't want to go. It wasn't right. The van door couldn't shut fast enough as sobs racked my body. One day the pain would be over.

September was full of wedding planning and turmoil in the Middle East. Emergency deployments loomed overhead. I tried not to imagine having to cancel the wedding because of a deployment. That seemed too horrible to be true. I immersed myself into choosing bridesmaid dresses, music, invitations, flowers and a million other things. Josh's dress blues needed to match everyone, so I threw out my dream of a lavender wedding and chose ruby red, a champagne hue and ivory. The color scheme was beautiful. The bridesmaids would wear floor-length red dresses and hold white carnations. I would wear white and hold a bouquet of red roses. The groomsmen would wear black suits with ivory ties. I listened to many songs, trying to choose the one in which I would walk down the aisle. Josh suggested, *Love is Not a Fight*, by Warren Barfield.

Love is a shelter in a raging storm
Love is peace in the middle of a war
And if we try to leave, may God send angels to guard the door
No, love is not a fight but it's something worth fighting for

It certainly wasn't traditional, but it told a story and was the heart of what we believed. It was also untraditional to have a wedding in a family life center, but it mattered more to us that we be married at our home church and in the building where we had first become friends than in a beautiful chapel somewhere else. The guest list just kept growing. The total ended up being over 500. We expected around 400 guests. The entire church was invited.

At the end of September, my family went to the coast again on our annual trip with my dad's family. On the way, we stopped by and saw Josh. It was two days before his trip to Alaska. We only had eight hours together, but it felt wonderfully long. We savored every moment of the day we had together, realizing that we wouldn't see each other until just before our wedding. "Goodbye" came in the same day "hello" had come.

Josh flew out to Alaska on his short deployment a couple days later. He had arrived in the sub-zero temperature wearing shorts. The cold air had been a shocker. He settled into his job. It was hard because he worked nights and had to walk to work. Thankfully, we could still see each other on Skype and could talk on the phone. We counted down the days.

There was a flurry of bridal showers in September and October. I had been to many showers in my childhood, tagging along with Mama, but the one at church was unlike any I had been to. It was packed with tables of gifts and food. I was overwhelmed with gratitude. Soaking in the moment, I promised never to forget what all these families had done for us. We filled our basement full of all the gifts.

The countdown to the wedding was ticking down. The final decisions were made. I missed Josh so much. It was bittersweet. I longed to see him and I prayed that time would fly straight to November 10th, but I also dreaded leaving my family. There was no way I could know or understand the pain of leaving them.

Clara and I were spending time together outside one day as autumn leaves danced in the trees. We sat down together on the grass. It was in the same spot Josh and I had sat and talked six months before in April.

"It's kind of mean."

I looked at her, confused. "What is mean?"

She looked away as her lip quivered. "It's just kind of mean that Josh wants to take you away. You belong to us, not him."

What could I say? How could I show her that Josh wasn't trying to be mean? She was only seven years old. It was so hard for her to understand.

"I want to go, honey. I will miss you so much, but I am supposed to go with him now."

Her dark eyes revealed the pain she felt. I pulled her to my chest, praying that God would help us both.

Each family member handled it differently. Some days, Daddy came into my room and sat on my bed. He would hold me close as though absorbing everything about me so that it wouldn't hurt so much. Mama never really let her feelings show to me, but I could still see them by the things she said and did. Kandace was my best friend. I couldn't imagine life without her. It was beyond heartbreaking for her. Sometimes she felt like I was abandoning her. We had many long, hard conversations about how I still loved her and always would. Clara dealt with it in her own unique way. Many red-rimmed eyes and lengthy hugs. Andrew didn't fully understand at first, but he began to, as the wedding day grew closer.

My last Sunday in the praise team came. The song's words got stuck in my throat. I gripped the microphone I had used for three years. It was time to turn it in, like turning in a key. I cried as I sang; everyone knew why.

The sun dipped below the horizon one of those last days. Through the window, Clara and Andrew ran up the hill to MaMaw and PaPaw's house. The TV was turned low, but I could still hear Fox News. The aroma of supper still lingered through the house. Wendy, my old kitty, climbed up the deck steps and lazily fell asleep.

Home. This place had been home since that day Kandace and I dashed through the door 11 years before and had fallen into our beds for our first night in the house. It held all of my memories. If the walls could have spoken, they could have proven it true.

Lord, how will I ever leave this place? I can't imagine a life other than this.

He would help me. Until the day came when all that I knew would change, I would hold onto all I had, savoring each second.

13 WEDDING DAY

The Coming Goodbye

The Alaska trip had mercifully ended in time for my fiancé to have a few days to recover from jetlag before his trip home for the wedding. There were so many things to think about with a couple days before the big day, but one thing was most important.

Josh would be here soon.

The church was looking beautiful. Lights strung across the ceiling of the reception room where the food would be placed. We had decided to have the ceremony and the reception in the same rooms, so there was a team of people assigned with the responsibility of turning a ceremony into a reception. I dreaded it, but Dad insisted that they had it down to a science. The re-set from the ceremony set-up to the reception set-up would be done in less than 20 minutes.

I ran over the list of things to do in my mind as I swirled lights and tulle around the white columns on stage. Balloons, flowers and runners were all ready. Food was going to be hors d'oeuvers and I had little to do with that. Dress was cleaned. Everyone had his or her clothes. Susan Sturgill, our director, was doing a fabulous job of handling all the details.

It was going to be good. I just wanted to see Josh.

My back was turned to the door as I worked on stringing more lights near the back of the church. Mama turned abruptly. I whisked around to see Josh running toward me, his arms opened wide. He picked me up off of my feet.

Together and no more goodbyes.

I had never understood when people talked about true love. The love that goes so deep and is willing to give up everything to keep it was always a mystery to me. But with Josh by my side, I understood it. Suddenly, nothing else mattered. If there were only ten people at the wedding, my dress was soiled and the cake fell, it would all be perfectly fine.

We got our marriage certificate at the courthouse and took it to Daddy. That trip made it all so real.

Friday morning we pulled everything together and finished up all that had to be done at the church. All the details were falling into place. Josh and I hung bows on each door at the church. We laughed and joked about how crooked they were. Anticipation was building for the rehearsal dinner that night. I tried desperately to relax and not overwork myself, but Josh had other plans. He told me goodbye in the early afternoon and went mountain biking. I don't know what possessed me to agree to let him go. One last adventure before the wedding was hard to turn down I guess. But I spent the whole afternoon worrying that he would fall off a cliff or break a bone.

It was all moving so quickly. Everything would be over in less than 24 hours. I would be married. Before going home from church to get ready for the rehearsal, I sneaked over to the old prayer chapel. The sanctuary was bright inside as the afternoon sun shown through the stained glass windows. The musty smell of being infrequently used made me miss the years I had sat on the second pew from the piano on the left side – with my family. I had been a little thing, in the prime of childhood before we had moved into the larger family life center building. The old piano beckoned me to play. Shaking off the pressure, the change and all that was about to come, I sat down on the squeaky bench. The colorful light bathed my face as the slightly out of tune notes met my ears. I closed my eyes and played with all of my heart. My voice raised and music filled every inch of the sanctuary. Tears rolled as I worshiped. There was only God and me and I rested in that moment.

Those few moments are a treasure to me. My life would soon pick up speed and be nearly impossible to slow down.

Hours later, I smoothed out my blue, lacy dress and twisted my hands impatiently as I waited for everyone to arrive for the rehearsal. Everything looked lovely and I was so pleased. Once everyone had hugged and chatted for a while, we began the rehearsal. I hadn't given a lot of thought to the details of how the ceremony would flow; yet, my daddy, mama and Susan had. When someone asked me a question and I shrugged, one of the three came to my rescue. No one had told me it would be so complicated. Everyone followed directions and suddenly I was walking down the aisle with Daddy. Josh wouldn't look up as I walked toward him. When I asked why, he said, "I want tomorrow to be the first time … when it's real." The music was perfect and each groomsmen and bridesmaid floated down the aisle. It was easy considering there were only four of each. Kandace, Taylor, Leah and my dear friend Jessica Hall were my bridesmaids. Josh had chosen his four best friends as his groomsmen, all from different chapters of his life … each a blessing and encouragement to him.

We ate and cut the groom's cake. To be funny, we had decided to get a cake that was half light blue and half dark blue. Considering my family is avidly North Carolina fans and my fiancé is passionately a Duke fan, it suited well. Everyone had a good laugh when Daddy ate a piece from the Duke side and Josh ate a piece from the North Carolina side.

While we ate cake, videos I had made with pictures from our lives played on screens in the church. It was a sentimental moment to reflect on how far we had come and how much God had blessed us. We gave a small speech and thanked everyone for coming.

Then it was over.

Everyone told me how excited they were for tomorrow. I couldn't believe the night was ending. Tomorrow was the day. It was hitting me so strongly.

I gave the church one last, thorough look-thorough and found everything perfect. Josh lingered until we all had to leave. He grasped my hands and said sweetly, "The next time I will see you …"

"I'll be walking down the aisle," I finished.

There in that moment, all the waiting swelled up and boiled over. This was the last goodbye as two unmarried people. All that pain of missing him was going to be gone. My chest twisted with a bitter-sweetness as Clara stuck as close to me as she could.

I can't have it all.

It seemed like everyone in my contact list on my phone was texting me. The bridesmaid shoes Kandace had insisted on were impossible to walk in, so I spent a while digging through my closet for black heels. I checked on everyone's attire and made certain that Clara had her flower basket and Andrew had his ring pillow. I smoothed out my dress and veil and tried to breathe.

We sat as a family in the living room before bed for the last time. Clara and Andrew hugged me so tightly, I feared I would burst. I kissed them both and pulled the covers to their necks.

Memories of that night are shadowy. Perhaps the magnitude of the next day makes my wedding eve cloudy. I just remember tears in my throat and packing my honeymoon bag. One distinct memory has settled into my mind, never to leave.

I stood by my bed with my bags packed, every moment of my journey playing in my head. Could this really be my last night at home? I was still such a child, so naive, so innocent and I knew it. My stomach loosened its knots when I lifted my face to the ceiling. God's soft whisper was like a wind.

You are exactly as I want you to be. Well done, child. I'm proud of you.

I slept deeply.

The First Kiss

The phone was ringing.

"Hello?" I answered.

"Hey baby, I'm so sore!"

My mind was like a train trying to start its engine and pull those wheels into motion. I was so sleepy. What was today? Why is he sore?

My WEDDING!

I am getting married today!

He is sore from bicycling!

"Did you hear me?" he asked.

"I heard you. Good morning to you too! And happy wedding day!"

"Yes, you too! But I am so sore!"

Why hadn't I refused to let him go? "Well, I'm sorry. You think you'll make it through the day?"

"Yes." Someone yelled for him in the distance. "I love you and I'll talk to you later."

Thus ended our conversation.

Mama and Kandace had already gone to the church. They had wanted me to sleep a few extra minutes. It was before seven a.m. and the wedding wasn't until one o'clock. Hair and makeup was supposed to take hours, so all of the girls had to arrive very early.

When I had checked all of my bags several times, taken a shower and thrown on some sweat clothes, I walked down my stairs for the last time. Daddy was in the kitchen. He was wearing that sweatshirt he always wore.

"Let me help you carry those out," he said.

The sun glistened off of the frozen dew. The sky was already as blue as it could be.

Daddy scraped the ice off of the windshield of my car after putting all of my bags in the back seat. I watched him as though for the first time. This man was about to give me away. This man who had given everything to me. In that moment, I realized so clearly how all that ever mattered to me was him … was my family. No amount of vacations, clothes, gifts and things could amount to what he and Mama had given me. They had given me themselves. There stood my daddy. He had protected me and loved me so faithfully and so perfectly. How many times had I taken him for granted? I wanted to bury my face in his chest and never let go.

What a privilege it had been to hold the last name "Brown" for 18 years. Though I knew my last name would change in a few hours, my heart wouldn't. Every value, moral, memory and truth he and Mama had engraved on my heart would always be there. They had done their jobs and had done it so well.

Thank you, Lord. Thank you for parents so wonderful that I could never have deserved them.

I did bury my face in his chest as the birds tweeted their songs and the breeze blew softly.

"I love you, Kate."

"Oh, I love you, Daddy!"

The drive to church was my last few moments alone. I spent them praying, taking deep breaths and enjoying the excitement of the day.

The room upstairs was bustling. Makeup and hair accessories were everywhere. I hugged each of my bridesmaids and we talked and enjoyed ourselves. Josh brought us breakfast, but he had one of the girls go get it from him so that I couldn't see him, but I heard his voice.

Mama wisped the airy dress over my head and laced it up. I spun around for all the girls as they admired. Everyone looked gorgeous. We were all ready and it was time for pictures. I just did everything I was told and soaked in each moment. There were smiles all around. It was picture perfect and if the wedding was nearly as wonderful as the moments before, then all would be wonderful.

"It's a few minutes until show time!" Kandace bellowed.

I smacked my lips together with one last coat of lip-gloss.

Almost time.

I was about to kiss for the first time. That one thought just kept rising to the top. A million butterflies were poured into my chest and stomach. As a little girl I had always wondered if I would have cold feet or apprehension before my wedding, but there I stood so perfectly at peace. Not a doubt on my mind.

Each member of my family hugged me and headed downstairs. All except Mama, she was still upstairs and it was past time for her to go downstairs. She calmly explained that Josh was waiting on his dad to arrive. I fought back frustration. We had known that this would be a possibility. Josh must have been stressed; this was his only worry. Everyone told me it was going to be okay.

We were several minutes after 1 o'clock when I was told we were ready to go. Everyone was there. Mama kissed me on the cheek and left us. It was just the five of us girls. I wasn't sure when to go behind the church even though someone was supposed to come tell us. I wasn't going to be late, so I rallied the other four and we happily took off downstairs where we were met by a few straggling guests. I tried to hide myself as I slipped around the back of the church, but my large, white dress was unmistakable.

We sneaked in the reception room where the bridesmaids were supposed to enter. They would walk down the far left of the three aisles. The groomsmen were supposed to be on the other side, coming down the right aisle. I didn't have time to worry about if they were actually over there.

Then I realized that people could see me in that room. I saw the tables behind me and squatted down under them, laughing at the odd moment. The music began for my wedding party to enter. The Hall sister's string trio sounded beautiful as they played *Jesu' Joy of Man's Desiring*. I had chosen it because my mama and daddy had done so for their wedding 22 years before.

Light flooded the room as Daddy came to retrieve me from my hiding place. We stood behind the back door of the church. I gripped his arm and looked into his eyes. The sun was warm on my back as he said, "This is it!"

It was too surreal to be happening, but it was. When the music reached the exact, perfect moment, I nodded that the doors should open. Hundreds of eyes fell on us as we entered. There were rose petals under my feet as I walked. Sweet murmurs as I passed by friends. I couldn't see Josh yet, but I would as soon as I turned the corner.

The music reached it's crescendo as his eyes met mine. I walked slowly, taking in each blessed second. His eyes glistened with tears and his jaw was firmly set. My bridesmaids in red, so beautifully lined to one side and Josh's fine groomsmen, all lined beside him, made for the perfect picture.

Daddy spoke to us and the congregation. Then Daddy grasped my hand and pulled it to Josh's. He was giving me away. We stepped onto the stage holding hands. We exchanged our vows and promised to love forever and always, for better or worse. Both of us had written a letter to one another. Josh isn't a writer like I am, but his words sounded as though nothing more beautiful could have ever been said. The words were so easily spoken, that I imagined he had longed to say them forever.

The rings. The unity sand we mixed. The music. The prayers. It all fell perfectly into place. The room was bursting with love, joy and a miracle that was soon approaching.

"Here comes the moment you have all been waiting for!" Daddy proudly said. "Katy is now going to give her very first kiss away."

Josh looked at Daddy, his eyes begging for the coming words.

"Josh, you may now kiss your bride."

It was slow motion. This moment I had imagined for years. This moment that many said was an impossible destination, a foolish dream. This instant when the symbol of my purity would be proclaimed. I had arrived. My heart was unbroken and still in one piece, thanks be to God and only God. It was time to give it away. The wait was over. The blessing of saving my kiss was about to be received … and given.

My heart sped as Josh put his hand on my neck. Leaning in, I felt a wave of pure desire wash over me. I knew what to do even if it wasn't going to be perfect.

We kissed.

It was worth it.

It was undoubtedly worth the wait. Yes, that wait which had been a lot harder than I had imagined. It was worth each step of that journey. What of that piece of paper I had ripped to shreds years before? The paper that had said, "I love you." Maybe, just maybe, I was meant to love Josh from the very beginning. Perhaps my heart even knew it so long ago. However, I had tried so desperately to awaken that love at the wrong time. Solomon said in

Song of Solomon 2:7, "I adjure you, O daughters of Jerusalem, by the gazelles or the does of the field, that you not stir up or awaken love until it pleases." Love at the wrong time isn't true love. Years ago, in my own moment of pain and hurt as I had ripped the paper apart, weeping uncontrollably, God had been saving me. Through the pain, I was rescued. It seemed to be a pattern in my life. This pattern where I faltered and He always picked me up. His timing was so much more perfect than mine, and in that moment I knew it was so very true.

"May I now present to you for the first time in modern history, Mr. and Mrs. Joshua Isaacs!"

The old wedding march started perfectly on cue and filled the room as we bounded down the aisle. We kissed again outside the doors. I didn't realize how many cameras snapped pictures. My family and close friends joined us outside. It began to sink in as we embraced each one. Gathered together, we were positioned and posed for pictures. Meanwhile, the crowd went outside and into the fellowship hall to wait until the huge auditorium space was transformed into a reception hall. When we came back inside, I was amazed at the amount of people setting up. Balloons, flowers, food, tablecloths, and all other little details were swarming into place.

Josh just held me close and I just kept on smiling.

Mama rushed me upstairs to bustle up my dress and I freshened up. I heard Steve Bryan, who had been Daddy's old roommate in college and had remained a dear friend, calling each name of the wedding party. Applause increased when Josh and I entered. I couldn't help but dream of the Church finally being married to the Bridegroom (Jesus) when we are all called in Heaven to the Marriage Supper. This was only a taste.

Speaking of tasting, the cake was high on its table. The ivory, round, three-layer cake was just beautiful. I surveyed the room and was thrilled at how quickly and easily it had been transformed to look so good. Later Daddy told me that it had taken 15 minutes – even less time than they had assumed.

The reception was honestly a blur and way too fast for the memories to sink in. I hugged a couple hundred people and managed to eat a grape and half of a cracker in between. Josh and I danced and then Daddy and I danced. It would be safe to say that Daddy and I probably failed the dancing aspect as we swung slopping spins to "My Girl."

We cut the cake and made a mess. Hugged more people. I threw the bouquet and Josh threw the garter.

Boom, boom, boom. It was all happening so quickly.

Daddy walked by our table a few minutes later. "It's about time to leave."

"Now?!" I said, shocked.

"Yes," he answered, with his pastoral, leadership voice.

The room cleared quickly and everyone went outside. Josh and I were directed to walk through the throng of people and kiss halfway.

Probably one of my favorite moments of the whole day was when we stepped outside the door. Streamers and floating balloons, mixed with happy faces and noise. I loved every face I walked by. What love filled the air. Kissing heartily, Josh leaned me slightly back. Everyone whooped.

The car was all decked out and Josh's door handle was covered in shaving cream. It took him a few tries to get the door opened. Dozens of balloons floated out of the car. I gave the groomsmen a jokingly evil glare. Daddy helped us clear the car as he claimed that balloons could cause us to wreck. *Oh Daddy!*

The crowd waved and yelled as we got in the car. Josh put it in reverse and the cans clanked. When we were about to turn out of the parking lot, I turned back. Balloons were soaring in the wind above the church and the crowd was still there all talking and laughing.

Thus concluded our wedding … and my dream.

The Honeymoon and Thereafter

All I remember about the drive to our honeymoon destination was a fierce headache, nasty Mexican food, and confusing directions.

Mama had kindly printed out the directions, but I didn't even look at them with my head pounding from the excitement and exhaustion. Josh just merrily drove along the dark, curvy roads while I dozed. The drive was much longer than I had expected, probably because we went way out of the way. When we pulled in front of the cabin, none of that mattered anymore. The cabin was rustic and quaint, yet still luxurious.

My headache ebbed away. The night was beautiful. Everything was worth the wait. The next morning, the light filled the cabin and I could see the majestic mountains from the bedroom. We stepped out on the front porch together and breathed deeply. It was my first day as a wife and I felt like nothing could shake me. Oh, but the coming days would be difficult. This unstoppable newlywed couple would have to learn that they weren't so powerful on their own. Challenges were ahead, but for a while, ignorance was bliss. I only cared about all I had right then ... all I had waited for my whole life. Marriage was all I had dreamed it would be ... and more.

14

FOR BETTER OR FOR WORSE

Back to Reality

There I was. Josh and I sat side by side in one of the many gray buildings on base.

"Mr. and Mrs. Isaacs?"

Josh nudged my arm. I hadn't recognized my new name. The lady who had said it stood behind us. I could already tell I didn't like this place. Everything about this base was stiff and unfriendly. We were given directions to our townhouse and handed keys. Josh carried me over the threshold as we laughed gaily. When he put me down I gave the room a hard lookover. It wasn't too bad. The walls were as white as the hospital walls were a hundred years ago, but other than that, it was pretty nice. We stood in the middle of the living room, holding hands and prayed over our new home. Our first home. A peace washed over me as we bathed the bare house in prayer.

Havelock, North Carolina was a little postage stamp of a town. I thought it rather ugly and gray. It was military all the way with lots of places to drink alcohol, grab fast food and get a tattoo. Since the town was not the rolling, Blue Ridge Mountains I had left, I wanted to make my home quaint and homey to make up for the lack of beauty around me. It would be a while before I could even try to make the house a home. That first night in our house, I fixed lasagna, using most of the dishes I had managed to force into the car. Mama and Daddy were bringing the rest of our belongings in a few days; until then, we would make do. I flipped a plastic storage box over and used it as a table for our meal. That night, we spread a blanket on the floor in our bedroom and fell asleep from exhaustion.

Like many newlyweds, we didn't have much those first few weeks … and months. I did all I could to make do. The house filled up when Mama and Daddy came down with all of our things, but no matter how many pictures I hung, rugs I laid or furniture we bought, it didn't fill the ache in my chest. I missed my bedroom. I longed for the scent of my home.

That's when it began.

Any little thing would flip the switch and I would be hunkered over sobbing. I missed Andrew's arms around my waist before bedtime and his lips on my cheeks with his wet kisses. What was Kandace doing at night since I wasn't there to sit and chat? Did Mama accidently call me to come set the table, forgetting I wasn't there? I wondered if Clara ever walked up to my room and stood there, trying to remember what used to be. And Daddy … did he ever look down at the piano and long for the music I had played?

I pushed up the windows each morning after Josh went to work and let the sound of children playing float through the house. My fingers ached, missing the ivory keys. On Sunday morning, church went on at home without me. I tried to remember how Mama cooked and what she had said about not washing dark clothes with white clothes. I knew all of those things, but they were suddenly all jumbled up in my brain, just when I needed to remember them.

Most nights I cried myself to sleep. Josh told me it would be okay. He tried to comfort me, but he didn't understand. Every day I was alone for hours while Josh was at work because we only had one car. After years of constant noise and activity, there was now silence. The wedding was obviously over and my life was spiraling down in depressed anxiety. Sometimes, my weary husband misunderstood my tears and asked why he wasn't enough. I quickly tried to explain that he was enough, but missing home was natural.

But was this natural? Marriage was proving to be much more difficult than I had ever imagined. No one had prepared me for this and no one could have. I didn't like anything around me except for my husband. And sometimes he wondered if I liked him.

I didn't lack for things to do. I wrote, organized the house, taught piano, studied and various other things. Some said I would struggle because I hadn't graduated from college before I had gotten married. Others told me that I needed a full time job. None of those things would have filled the hole in my life. I was dissatisfied and jobs and education wouldn't fix my discontentment.

I began to despise our house. The quietness mocked me. It was reminding me of the nights I had laid in bed as a child, when the dark quiet had been a place of fear and pain. The quiet was so dark. It was better when it was filled with children and noise and good, happy things. Here I was facing fear again. Would my life always be this lonely?

One day, adrenaline coursed through my veins. I slammed both hands against the wall of our house, rattling the pictures. Choking sobs escaped me lips. Those sobs morphed into moans. I had never been one to take out my frustration in a physical way, but beating the walls with my fists that day, I felt the pent up tension slowly release. As I screamed at my house and asked God where He was, I began to realize something.

You wrestle not against flesh and blood … or walls.

The words from the end of Ephesians. I was fighting something larger than myself. I was fighting against the spiritual forces of evil. Those walls weren't my enemy and neither was this miserable town.

With my red face pressed against the cold, tiled floor, I felt just enough of God's presence to know He was still there. He hadn't left. But in my hatred of all that was around me, in my confusion and loneliness, I had lost sight of Him.

I didn't feel myself being pulled out of the pit, but I felt a bit of light fill my heart. Over a few weeks I cried less and smiled more. Josh took me to buy a keyboard and it filled the house with all of the music I had missed. It was therapy for my soul. Josh and I grew in our relationship. We had seen "for better" and "for worse" and we had come through a dark valley. God had never left us. And when more valleys came, we would remember the way.

Deployment

Scarlett O'Hara said in *Gone With the Wind*, "I can't think about that right now. If I do, I'll go crazy. I'll think about that tomorrow."

My motto was nearly those exact words. I had never been one to "put off" worrying, but when it came to deployment it was too great a fear to even ponder. Josh and I had truly become a family. The military didn't really care. He had a job to do. I knew the long awaited deployment to Afghanistan in June was quickly approaching. So to comfort myself, I decided that I wasn't allowed to worry about it until after our Mexico mission trip in April. Josh and I joined the team from our home church at Mt. Pleasant and headed off to Weslaco, Texas in mid April. I was thrilled that Josh would get to experience a mission trip like I had been able to do for years. He loved every second and poured out his heart to the boys there. He even led one to receive Jesus as his Savior. I turned 19 years old on the trip and the team celebrated it with a big cake and a hearty singing of, "Happy Birthday!"

All too soon it was over and Josh and I were driving back to Cherry Point. We missed the team and the people and the miracles God had done in each life. With the completion of the trip came the crushing realization, "I am supposed to worry now." It sounds ridiculous, yet it was my constant thought.

God never said, "Pray and I'll keep him there with you." In fact, I never heard God's voice at all. In a way, I felt like the Marines had some power that even God didn't care to deal with. I knew better, but I felt like God was detached from the military world. After the lonely darkness I had experienced, it seemed that this place was spiritually desolate. Yet again, I knew better; God was all around me. He was hidden in the small things and ordinary days.

I began praying that Josh wouldn't have to go on the deployment. I would still love God and thank Him even if Josh had to go, but I saw no harm in asking for this miracle. As the time drew nearer, Josh stopped offering the words of encouragement and comfort and just "laid it out."

"I have to go. It won't change."

"Ahh, it will if God allows. Your superiors may think they have all the power, but they don't. They will do God's will without even knowing it."

One night, I began to feel my hopes caving in. The deployment was becoming an idol in my life. I cried out to God, sobbing on Josh's chest.

Oh Lord Jesus, I'm done. I can't take it anymore. It's in Your hands.

The next morning Josh came home for lunch. He leaned against the wall with his hands in his pockets.

"I was told to come home and tell you that I do not have to go on the deployment to Afghanistan. They want me to stay back."

We clung to each other. I cried the first tears of joy in a long time. God had chosen to answer our prayers with the answer we so desperately wanted.

A few days later, Josh was informed that he would have to go on a five to six week long deployment to Arizona in July. It was so much better than the alterative that it hardly affected me at all.

My family offered to let me stay with them those weeks. The few days before Josh left, he drove me home and we went to the waterfall where he asked me to marry him. We relished each last moment together. It came time to tell him goodbye. I thought my heart would break, though I kept telling myself that it wasn't so long. He drove down the driveway like I had done that day of our wedding. I felt how Daddy must have felt when I drove away. He must have known because as soon as I turned around, he was there to pull me into his arms.

I was extremely excited when I realized that I would get to go to the Fine Arts Summer Academy in Nashville with my family. I even got to sing in the choir at the final show, which was at the Grand Ole Opry. Kandace got a solo. She dressed in a long, white dress. Standing in the middle of the stage, with a crowd and orchestra behind her, she sang *Down to the River*. Her organic, smooth voice drifted over the audience and captured every listener. It was glorious.

Not every day of that deployment was glorious. Several weeks later, I dug my toes into the dewy, late morning grass outside the fence of Daddy and Mama's garden. Bugs humming and hazy August heat drifting. I pressed my cell phone tightly against my ear, pointing my head higher, hoping for a better signal. I gripped the garden's solid gate and swallowed hard. My husband had said that same sentence again over the phone. It rang in my ears like a gong.

"We are strong; you know we are."

But knowing and feeling are two different things. I was thankful that only the schizophrenic cat at my feet could see me swiping tears. When we both hung up I couldn't decide if I wanted to wither in the damp grass below and cry or sniff back those miserable sobs and run inside.

I began, unknowingly, to do what I often did when nothing else could help.

Love lifted me.
Love lifted me.
When nothing else could help, love lifted me.

Singing the words from my childhood soothed the ache. I twisted the white gold wedding band on my finger and lifted my face to the blue country sky. I remembered that though I was a speck on rolling mountains – one person in a world of billions – I was a precious gem in the hands of the King, bought at a great price. The enemy of fear fled as God whispered, "I'll never let you go." His words were as soft as the wind through the tall oaks. "I am strong, child. You know I am."

Baby Clothes

"I need to pick up another baby shower gift," I told Josh one day several weeks after our one year anniversary.

"Okay. That's fine," he said as he flipped the light off to go to sleep.

"Another baby gift …." I said slowly to emphasize my irritation.

I didn't want to be frustrated that I needed to buy another happy couple a gift, but I felt like I had bought enough baby gifts to stock Babies "R" Us. The cheery couple lived nearby and was having a boy. They had already chosen a beautiful name. I looked back at Josh as a jealous chill seeped over me.

"Are you listening to me?"

He finally looked at me. "Yes, get a gift"

I went and got a gift. I wondered why it didn't seem to faze Josh. Was it supposed to faze me? Why was it so hard to go to baby stores and rub soft blankets and squeeze the cute stuffed animals? Why was it breaking my heart?

The precious little, blue outfit would look perfect on an infant. Instead of checking out immediately, I wandered through the car seats and cribs. Once I was home I gently wrapped the gift. Tears began to roll down my face.

Why can't I ever take the tags off? Because, they aren't for my baby.

It was what I wanted. I want to say that the clothes and bottles and gifts … all of them, were for my baby. Why did they always have to be for someone else? I sobbed as I looked up, willing my eyes to see through the ceiling and past the sky into the heavens where the Sovereign God sat.

"Oh God, where is my baby?"

Panic welled in my chest. What if I never have a baby? What if something is wrong? Why do all of these other women get to live near their families and go to the church that they choose and still be blessed with children? I was the one who was far from home and my extended family. If anyone needed a family of her own … it was me.

"Please God, you know my heart. I don't want to be jealous, I don't want to covet, but didn't You say that children are a blessing from You? Didn't You say that the man who has many is blessed? Are you withholding this blessing?"

Josh and I went to a store the following Saturday. I walked down the aisles of the baby clothes. A soft blue pair of pajamas caught my eye. Beside of it was a pink, baby girl version. I pulled them off the racks and Josh followed me as I bought our children clothes.

I sat on the bed and ripped the tags off as joy beat along with my heart. I held each pajama separately and caressed the downy softness. My throat lurched with tears as I reminded myself that regardless of whether I had a boy or girl first, one of the tiny outfits I held would be worn. It felt good to hold on to an absolute. I could say that these were my baby's clothes, not someone else's.

The baby clothes were washed and hung in my closet with my clothes. Every day I touched them and occasionally I even held them against my chest. Months passed and more friends gave birth to daughters and sons. Bitterness threatened to take over my mind each time I saw a new picture on social media or when another person asked why I hadn't had a baby yet.

Josh was so good with children. He smiled and waved at each baby he saw and the babies generally waved right back at him. I felt like I was withholding from him something he really wanted … children. Sometimes he would say, "I can't wait to have a son or daughter." For months I laughed and agreed, but as the seasons came and went, I would nod and quickly walk away to cry. He longed to be a father, but not like I longed to be a mother. The loneliness of being 300 miles from any family I had ever known, fed the desire to have my very own family. Imagining Josh thousands of miles away and myself sitting alone in base housing made me tremble with sadness.

Each lonely afternoon, I continued opening my windows and letting the sound of children playing on the playground across the road fill the house. Their bicycles and scooters zoomed by and their laughs and happy squeals made me smile. I took long walks around the park. Most of the women I passed were either swelling with pregnancy or had a small baby in a stroller. I wondered if every-one had children or if women like me just worked jobs or stayed indoors. Whatever the reason, all I knew was that every woman I saw had a passel of precious children. As time went by, I quit my walks and closed my windows. The sounds that used to be very sweet were now bittersweet and I feared that if I kept listening, they may have turned bitter altogether.

I involved myself in volunteering at two pregnancy care centers. I didn't realize that it could easily turn into a form of torture. But I was happy to find that I enjoyed the time I spent with new friends and doing useful activities. Yet, seeing women who didn't really want a baby made my heart hurt. I knew that their circumstances were different from mine, so they didn't see the blessing that each child is. Even if one is conceived in less than good circumstances, God still has a purpose for each one. These mothers don't always know this, but that's why we are there ... to tell them. I focused on pushing aside my own feelings.

In those months, I thought of couples I had known throughout my childhood. Those particular couples had never been able to have a child. Some of them had chosen adoption and others had decided to not go that route. Sometimes the Holy Spirit guided my mind away from myself and whispered that I should pray for others who were like us and for those who had waited much longer than we had. When I prayed, I felt His peace.

Am I or am I not in control?

It was that small familiar voice. He was soft and gentle as He asked me the question that seemed unreasonably hard to answer. God was in control, but I wondered, "Why can't He just let the blessings fall now? Why do others get the good end of the deal while we are supposed to accept that He has a reason for why we wait?"

You haven't experienced all that they have gone through.

Maybe they dealt with burdens I never had to carry.

I was thankful for that reminder, but as more time passed, I felt my hope slipping. Each time someone asked us why we didn't have a baby yet, I would swallow angry comebacks. People somehow assumed it was all because we didn't want a baby, when that was actually all we wanted.

I felt myself swinging back down into a valley of pain as I began going to the doctor for treatment. The military hospital seemed to only want to do what was absolutely necessary and this wasn't necessary. It took weeks to get results on tests and answers to questions.

One Sunday, the pastor at our church preached about "faith." He said what I had been told all of my life: "If you have the faith of a mustard seed, it will move mountains. Believe that it is so even when it isn't so, so it will become so."

I thought hard on that. Faith. Was that the missing ingredient? I didn't want to bribe God. It was His will ... but maybe He was waiting on me to stop wondering and have faith. One night in mid December, I looked over at Josh and asked, "Do you believe if we pray in faith, that God will answer our prayers?"

"Yes," he responded, "if it is His will."

"I believe it is and we just haven't shown the faith."

That night we prayed. It was different from any other prayer I had prayed. On my knees on the cold, hard floor, I poured out my heart to God. We prayed together, tears mingling together, begging God for a miracle. With "amen" we stood up and breathed a sigh in unison. Everything was going to be wonderful. God had heard and would answer.

We went home for Christmas and had a wonderful visit. There was so much joy and pleasure in my favorite holiday. Lights, Fraser Firs, sweet treats, laughter, hugs, and old music filled every corner of every house. This Christmas was uniquely beautiful, because when I looked into my husband's eyes, I saw a bond and a love that we had only begun to tap into a year before. We were finally so solid and comfortable in each other. Only time could grow such depths of trust and love. I could only imagine in wonder at what the future would hold.

The next few weeks were long. I had a doctor's appointment, where they loaded me full of plans and tests I could do if nothing happened soon. I refused to believe that "nothing would happen." It *would* happen.

I dropped by Josh's work on base and told him everything the doctor had said. My husband sat across from me in the dusty warehouse. It was just the two of us since he was on warehouse duty. He looked into my eyes and gripped my hands, "We have to have faith, Kathryn. You are pregnant."

My heart lurched at those wonderful words. He was right. Why was I doubting?

Faith. Have faith.

Tears filled my eyes, "You're right. I am."

Silence From Heaven

Time passed, gruelingly.

I went to volunteer at the pregnancy care centers like I had been doing the last couple months. The many prenatal books, pregnancy pamphlets, baby clothes were all lined up so fresh and perfect. So many ladies had bellies large in pregnancy. People had those familiar questions, "Do you have any children? Do you want any?" It was all so much. But I forced myself to remember the faith. I created the perfect plan to tell everyone the good news.

I was doing it – believing it was so, even when it wasn't, so it would become so.

Finally, I decided when I would find out whether we were going to have a baby. I felt that it would have been long enough. Josh didn't worry … or at least he never showed it. I held on to every shred of hope, knowing and proclaiming this was it.

The morning came. Shaking with anticipation, I felt an odd sense of peace.

I laid the test aside and set my clock. How many times had I done this? How many times had I waited just like this? I smiled, believing that the answer would be sure. God wouldn't let me down.

One expects a miracle moment. The positive test and joy filled tears of thanksgiving. That was how I would have written my story.

Negative.

As negative as it could be.

No tears. Nothing. No sound from heaven. No flooding of graceful mercy to wash over my pain. Silence. Loneliness so deep it struck my core.

With a stone face, I pulled my baby pajamas off of the small hangers in the closet. I pressed them against my chest as I sank down under the covers on our bed.

Rocking back and forth, the soft weeping overtook. I started talking.

"I am sorry, baby. I was trying to get you here. I believed it wasn't too much longer. I'm sorry I can't be your mama yet. I'm so sorry I can't hold you right here. I tried, baby. But, I'm not giving up. I never will."

God Is Always Good

I wasn't foolish enough to think God wasn't there or that He didn't see me and know what was going on. I just didn't understand why He would tell us to ask, to have faith and what we ask will be done. I wondered how could He say that if He doesn't answer. Part of me said: It's just another month. Get over it. But part of me ached with the question, *Why?* I realized that millions of God's children have asked that question throughout the span of time.

Though it hurt, I had to admit a few things. For starters, God never says when He will answer us. He also doesn't always say how He will answer us. I hadn't been wrong to pray in faith. There hadn't been a sin in believing. The sin was thinking that I could pressure God out of His will and change His timing.

Though I knew the truth, the path through the dark valley grew longer. It was like fighting an invisible enemy. That enemy was undoubtedly Satan and his evil forces. Spiritual warfare was nothing new to Josh or me, but it always felt intense. Each night, Josh held me in his arms and prayed. He always thanked God more than he asked for things, but I encouraged him to pray for answers to our needs and our questions. He was unwavering. When I asked why God was so silent, Josh just said simply, "In His time."

Months passed. We prayed. We thanked God for His blessings and praised Him for who we know He is. We remembered that He hadn't failed us. Or I remembered.

We were sitting on the couch. I was overwhelmed with decisions regarding procedures and doctor appointments. Was all of this necessary? Should we wait longer before doing this or that? I begged Josh for advice.

His face told me more than I cared to know. He turned the TV off and looked at me.

"I am so sick of this."

For one moment, I was wondering if I had thought those words or he had said them. He had most certainly said them. That was something I would have said, not him. In my eyes, he was the faithful one.

"What do you want me to say?" he asked.

"Can't we pray?"

"We can, sure. But Kathryn, why?"

Why what? I had a strange feeling that I knew what he was going to say next.

"He doesn't answer us."

I had been right. I had thought that same thought so many times. Like a dark shadow, I felt the evil cloud of despair covering him. It threatened to pull me in with it. I felt the same way I imagined the people felt in the old Westerns, when an epidemic of scarlet fever had taken over the town. Everyone hid in their homes, holding their breath and praying that the sickness would stay away. Just when it seemed it was over, a family member would shiver with fever. When the clothes were pulled back, there were dark red marks across the glistening skin. They were contaminated. I had always gasped at the TV screen in horror. How had it managed to come in? What had they done wrong?

Looking at Josh, I felt like a disease in his heart had suddenly been revealed. How had it managed to come in? What had we done wrong?

As suddenly as those thoughts filled my mind, they fled. God answered in that very moment. I hadn't truly felt Him in some time, but I recognized Him.

Tell him what he has always told you.

"Everything will be okay." It wasn't much, but his eyes lightened with the plain, old sentence. I knew I needed to say something eloquent and intelligent, but I wasn't sure I could trust myself to say something that wouldn't make everything worse. "He isn't doing anything wrong just because He is being quiet. He wants us to trust Him. And maybe He is speaking after all, but we are too stubborn to listen. Either way, we need to rest in Him."

I saw mirrored in his eyes, the pain I felt in myself. Our faith was being tested. It was a critical moment.

From that moment nothing suddenly got easier. Our circumstances remained the same, but we felt a seed of peace and hope planted into lives. We moved forward in pursuit of medical answers, but the intense pressure that it was all on our shoulders relaxed. It was in God's hands. Though it was still difficult to utter, He had a reason. Josh fell to the floor, pulling me with him. We bowed down together before the God who had never left us. The Faithful One.

Over the next few weeks, we worried less and trusted God more. I didn't even care to know anymore. I just lived. Meanwhile, God was busy. In mid-March, I was exhausted and nauseous. I reasoned that it was all in my head and that I was tricking myself to believe I was pregnant. I refused to take another pregnancy test. Time kept passing and finally and surprisingly, Josh said, "You are being stubborn." I had found out too many times that I was not going to have a baby and I wasn't ready for more negative news. So, I waited a few more weeks until I couldn't ignore the signs.

The morning I chose to do the test, I felt a peace I had never experienced in our year and a half journey. My Bible App on my phone opened at my tap.

"And without faith it is impossible to please him, for whoever would draw near to God must believe that he exists and that he rewards those who seek him" (Hebrews 11:6).

Faith. Somehow, with that verse, I was confident in the answer I would receive. Prayers poured out of my lips.

I will praise You. I will praise You either way.

Positive.

I crumpled to the floor in a heap, crying tears of joy.

This is Only the Beginning.

The keyboard's keys almost knew what to play without my help. It was the song I had written in 2010, You're Enough. Pastor Brad, from my old home church had encouraged me to write songs. At first I had been irritated and thought: anything I wrote would sound bad. He told me to write anyway. That was when I thought about the words that had come to my mind when Daddy had been so sick in Ethiopia back in May of 2009. In that hot, dark room the words had come to my mind. Words have come to my mind my whole life, but not often with a melody. So sitting in my bedroom that spring night, I had pieced together the music and words that had settled into my heart a year before. The chorus had gone like this:

> *You're enough for me*
> *When tears are my offering*
> *Or when joy is my song*
> *I'll always sing, Jesus, You're all this heart needs.*
> *I will not be afraid*
> *I will not live in fear*
> *For you are my Savior and You're always near*

When I had completed the song I had embarrassingly wondered if I deserved to write such a song. After all, I hadn't been through anything that hard in my life. Then I remembered how each life is laced with pain and joys alike. Some are thread with more of one than another. Some lives show the pain more obviously and some lives don't show their struggle at all. Some lives seem to be filled with nothing but happiness. What if we really only knew the truth about each person with whom we came into contact?

Pastor Brad had liked the song and it had become a song that the church heard often. It gave me goose bumps when I heard nearly five hundred people singing the words God had given to me.

Four years later, I sang the same words again. Only this time, I was in the quiet of my little house. This time it was just for me.

Since I had written the song, I had come so far. I had learned so much.

The film of my life rolled before my eyes. Slowly, calmly, peacefully. I didn't see the darkness. I saw the light.

When I was afraid, I had been comforted.

When I was lost, I had been found.

I remembered Grandma Ruth and her Milky Ways. The playhouse filled with children's voices on hot summer days.

My dreams of Clara and pushing her on the swing. Her first smile when she knew we loved her.

And Josh. Oh the days of putting my heart out there on a limb, nearly losing it. Lying in the bed praying for my future husband and not being able to help but pray for Josh's future wife, asking God if it could be me.

Shredding my journals.

Remembering Daddy becoming a pastor and being so proud of him behind the pulpit. And Mama. Mama filling every chapter of my life, pouring herself into me everyday. Crazy Kandace and me. Best friends.

Seeing Andrew for the first time and having my heart captured by my brother. God's mercy and miracles as he was healed through the blessing of reconstructive surgeries.

Selfishness and pride melted by African love. Little dark hands clinging to me and unashamed worship and righteousness. My friends Oshe and Kadir.

Growing up flashed before my eyes. Choosing to really be different, all because God said to be. Feeling Him when I acted, played the piano and sang.

That May when I saw Josh again. Becoming his friend. Going to the mailbox everyday, looking for just one more letter from Parris Island.

And then seeing him again, and choosing to wait. Yes, I remember those tears as I prayed, "God hold my heart. Don't let me give it away too soon."

Some hard days wondering if it was all worth it and praying that I could one day say it was. Missing him so badly, I thought my heart would rupture and holding his hand when he came home.

Him calling me Kathryn and saying for the first time, "I love you."

The waterfall and a diamond ring. Waiting on that kiss and gritting my teeth against the urge.

The wedding day. Blue sky and cool air. Walking down the aisle and Daddy saying, "This is it." Over four hundred eyes on me, but only seeing the blue ones at the end of the aisle.

The kiss.

The feeling of such freshness, newness, pureness and absolute goodness. Knowing and showing that *it was worth the wait*.

Thinking it was all a breeze.

Learning that life wasn't easy as we moved 300 miles away. All those gray buildings.

Tears. Missing my family so much and wondering if anyone remembered me.

I so easily remember my pain and God's quiet voice comforting me.

Then there is the summer garden at my old house. Gripping the fence while I talked to my husband over a thousand miles away. His steady voice mixing with the breeze around me, "We're strong."

My Marine's arms around me again at last.

Baby clothes. Wanting to be a mommy. Not becoming one. Choosing to trust in God's timing, even as my heart ached. Being blessed when we gave it up to Him.

The memories, the images. They swirl around me. What do they all mean?

Following my heart would have led me down a broken road. Many wonderful testimonies come from dark pasts. Testimonies of redemption from broken places and scarred hearts are powerful stories. My husband's testimony is just that. But there is no shame in walking the unbroken road. There is no shame in being free of scars and baggage.

In the end, I can say one thing: God was faithful. He never left me ... not for a moment.

He was all I needed even when I didn't realize it. No love compares to His. He heals the broken heart and keeps the unbroken one safe from harm.

So, how can I end a story that isn't even complete yet? I can't. Life goes on and the journey continues. I rest, assured that God is faithful each step of the way. Until that day when my life is over, it's my choice whether I am faithful to Him. I pray that I will be, because ... it is worth it. It always has been.

ALSO FROM ENERGION PUBLICATIONS

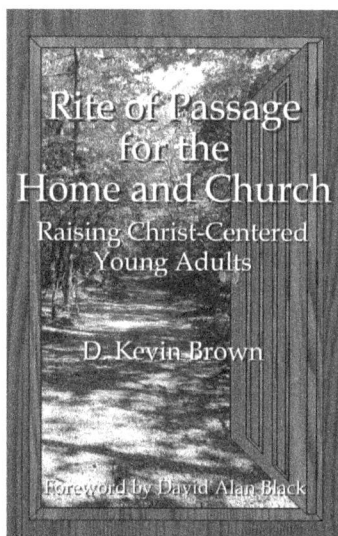

Rite of Passage for the Home and Church
Raising Christ-Centered Young Adults
D. Kevin Brown
Foreword by David Alan Black

For the first time people expected me to succeed and I was held responsible for my actions.

Alyssa
Rite of Passage Participant

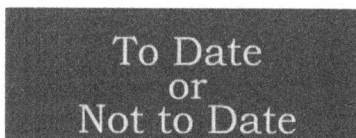

To Date or Not to Date
What the Bible Says about Premarital Relationships
D. Kevin Brown

Would you like to go for the gold in relationships? Here's some biblical help!

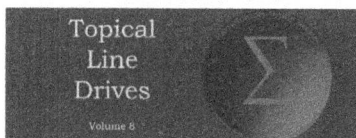

Topical Line Drives
Volume 8

MORE FROM ENERGION PUBLICATIONS

Personal Study

Holy Smoke! Unholy Fire	Bob McKibben	$14.99
The Jesus Paradigm	David Alan Black	$17.99
When People Speak for God	Henry Neufeld	$17.99
The Sacred Journey	Chris Surber	$11.99

Christian Living

It's All Greek to Me	David Alan Black	$3.99
Grief: Finding the Candle of Light	Jody Neufeld	$8.99
My Life Story	Becky Lynn Black	$14.99
To Date or Not to Date	D. Kevin Brown	$4.99

Bible Study

Learning and Living Scripture	Lentz/Neufeld	$12.99
From Inspiration to Understanding	Edward W. H. Vick	$24.99
Philippians: A Participatory Study Guide	Bruce Epperly	$9.99
The Caregiver's Beatitudes	Robert Martin	$4.99
Ecclesiastes: A Participatory Study Guide	Russell Meek	$9.99

Theology

Creation in Scripture	Herold Weiss	$12.99
Creation: the Christian Doctrine	Edward W. H. Vick	$12.99
The Politics of Witness	Allan R. Bevere	$9.99
Ultimate Allegiance	Robert D. Cornwall	$9.99
History and Christian Faith	Edward W. H. Vick	$9.99
The Journey to the Undiscovered Country	William Powell Tuck	$9.99
Process Theology	Bruce G. Epperly	$4.99

Ministry

Clergy Table Talk	Kent Ira Groff	$9.99
Out of This World	Darren McClellan	$24.99
Rite of Passage for the Home and Church	D. Kevin Brown	$13.99

Generous Quantity Discounts Available
Dealer Inquiries Welcome
Energion Publications — P.O. Box 841
Gonzalez, FL_ 32560
Website: http://energionpubs.com
Phone: (850) 525-3916

www.ingramcontent.com/pod-product-compliance
Lightning Source LLC
La Vergne TN
LVHW011156080426
835508LV00007B/429